CATHOLIC QUESTIONS, CATHOLIC ANSWERS

Catholic Questions, Catholic Answers

Father Kenneth Ryan

PUBLISHED BY ST. ANTHONY MESSENGER PRESS
CINCINNATI, OHIO

Cover design by Michael Andaloro

Published by St. Anthony Messenger Press
28 W. Liberty St.
Cincinnati, OH 45202
www.servantbooks.com

Printed in the United States of America
ISBN 0-89283-663-6 for Servant Publications edition.
ISBN 0-89283-701-2 for Catholic Digest Book Club edition.

04 05 06 07 27 26 25 24 23 22

Library of Congress Cataloging-in-Publication Data

Ryan, Kenneth, Father.
    Catholic questions, Catholic answers / Kenneth Ryan.
      p.   cm.
    ISBN 0-89283-663-6
    1. Catholic Church— Miscellanea.   I. Title.
BX1754.3.R93   1990
282—dc20   90-31065
                                                       CIP

Contents

Publisher's Preface

THE QUESTIONS AND ANSWERS IN THIS BOOK first appeared in Father Kenneth Ryan's column in the monthly magazine *Catholic Digest*, from 1981 to 1989. This column provides a monthly forum for inquiries about various facets of the Catholic faith. Hence, the particular selection of questions and answers in this book range from inquiries into the nature of God and Jesus' life and ministry to questions on particular Catholic devotions and practices such as the use of holy water and relics.

The questions have been largely shortened and personal references to the original questioner have been eliminated in the interest of the general popular reader. However, Father Ryan's original answers stand with minimal editing. With few exceptions, the author's answers are relatively short, providing the reader with a popular and accurate overview of a given issue, instead of an exhaustive, in-depth analysis.

Yet it is the publisher's belief that the sorts of issues raised in this book will be of compelling interest to Catholic readers, because they indicate the very real concerns of many American Catholics living the faith today. In that spirit, our hope is that the reader will find many of his or her own questions answered and gain a greater understanding of the Catholic faith within these pages.

CHAPTER ONE

GOD

Questions on explaining the Trinity,
the Holy Spirit in the Liturgy,
the gender of God,
and prayer to God the Father or Jesus.

God

Q. 1. I recently told a Jewish man that the Holy Spirit was the Third Person of the Holy Trinity and the Trinity was a mystery. What else should I have said?

A. That would depend on the depth of his interest. Quite possibly you told him enough for the present. The Trinity doctrine is the essence of the Catholic faith, but its relevance is best learned after other more familiar religious topics have been explored. The Church has forbidden philosophical "explanations" of the Trinity. But in a devotional sense, we can say that the Holy Spirit personifies the love between the Father and the Son. The Father is infinitely perfect. The Son is the Word of the Father, a perfect expression of the Father as the word of a human being is the expression of his thought. The Father perceiving the Son sees all perfection and loves the Son, as the Son sees and loves the Father. In simplified human terms we can say that this love is so intense (infinite, really) that as it proceeds from the Father and Son, it is personified in the Holy Spirit. He is a Person who is the love between the Father and the Son.

Another basic concept is that the Trinity was unknown to humanity before the revelation by Christ. Up to the time of Christ only the Father was known and obeyed. Christ revealed Himself as God ("I and the Father are one") so His followers knew both the Father and the Son during His life on earth. When the time came Christ ascended into heaven but sent the Holy Spirit upon the believers on Pentecost day. Thus, in the history of the world, men and women have known the Father, then the Father and the Son during the lifetime of Christ on earth, and now the Church knows the Holy Spirit and lives under His direction. It is because of this gradual revelation that the Church believes in the Trinity of the Father, Son, and Holy Spirit.

Q. 2. All our prayers in the liturgy are addressed to the Father or the Son. Doesn't this ignore the Holy Spirit?

A. It doesn't really. We are addressing the same God whether we say Father, Son, or Holy Spirit at the beginning of our prayer. But what you say is invariably true of the *Opening Prayer*, formerly called *Collect*, of the Mass.

For the first thousand years of the Church's existence, all the Collects were addressed simply to "God," *Deus* in Latin, but "through" Christ in the "unity" of the Holy Spirit. About the year 1000 there was a reaction to Arianism, which still cropped up from time to time. Arians regarded Christ as lower than the Father. The Catholic Church's reaction consisted in writing some of the new Collect prayers so that they were addressed, as you say, directly and personally to the Second Person. This was an affirmation of belief in the equality of the Son with the Father.

Really, it was not too good an idea because that word *through* then had to be dropped from the ending of the prayer. *Through* expressed a profound concept of the workings of the Blessed Trinity. God, the Creator, worked *through* the Second Person. The Nicene Creed says "through whom also He made the world." So, even though the Second Person is divine, He is also a man, and we go *through* Him to the Godhead in our official prayer. The Holy Spirit, the Third Person, was sent upon the Church by Christ to guide it and never has been thought of as a Mediator. So, in sending our prayers to the Godhead, we do not go *through* the Holy Spirit. Consequently He is never directly addressed in these official prayers. Of course, in non-official or devotional prayer there is not the same need to preserve doctrinal tradition and the Holy Spirit can be directly addressed.

All this is pretty well summed up in the Mass for Pentecost as now revised (1963). The Opening Prayer is addressed to "Almighty and ever living *God*"; the Responsorial Psalm's refrain is "Lord, send out Your spirit." The versicle before the Gospel is "Come, Holy Spirit, fill the hearts of Your faithful," a direct addressing of the Holy Spirit but not in so essential a part of the Mass as the ancient Opening Prayer.

Q. 3. Is it true that God does not have any gender and that the Holy Spirit is often referred to as "She"?

A. We human beings have only what is known as an analogical knowledge of God. We do not have complete, scientific, direct knowledge but can only try to understand the greatness of God, for instance, by the immeasurable universe. God's infinity we can never understand. God's attributes of love, mercy, justice and so on we can think of only as improvements on human love, mercy, and justice. We cannot imagine, much less know, such attributes when they are infinite. So whatever is good in maleness or in femaleness is found in God in infinite degree, as is every other attribute which to our human minds is good.

Christ referred to God as "Father" when teaching the Apostles the Lord's Prayer, but He could have been making allowance for the human limitation that makes us personify even the forces of nature as the old pagans did. Christ Himself was male, but while He was the culmination of God's revelation to the human race, even that revelation does not give us *complete* knowledge of God any more than the comparisons we make to get our analogical knowledge. Given the limitations of human intelligence, God would no more reveal Himself completely than He would lecture first graders on Einstein's theories.

Anyone who refers to the Holy Spirit as "She" probably has some mistaken notion that the Blessed Trinity is Father, Son, and Mother. That would be a new Christian heresy but would occur to people who think Mother Nature and God are the same. The Holy Spirit proceeds, according to the Nicene Creed, from the Father and the Son. The Son is not the offspring of the Father and the Holy Spirit. Even to think provisionally of the Holy Spirit as a mother or as a female is to contradict established Catholic belief. All in all, it is better to go along with the teaching method of our Lord and think of God as our Father in our prayers than to juggle theological abstractions every time we think of Him.

Q. 4. When I pray should it be to God the Father or Jesus? Doesn't a person have to pray to Jesus to get through to God the Father?

A. All the great Catholic mystics insist that the only way to union with God is through Jesus Christ, the God-Man.

Practically, of course, if yours is only a prayer of petition for some temporal favor, it doesn't matter whether you pray to God or Jesus. You would be pious in asking just a saint to intercede for you. But for the higher forms of prayer which have as their goal the perfect union of the human will with that of the Creator, the approach to the Creator must be through meditations on the life and teachings of Christ.

Muslims, Jews, Buddhists, Unitarians, and any religion which does not accept the divinity of Christ reject this approach, although some members of these faiths have reached very high states of natural prayer.

Some techniques are common to Christian and

non-Christian mystics, but the ultimate distinction between them is supernatural belief in the revealed doctrine of the Blessed Trinity, according to which Christ is God. The God whom all mystics seek is far above and beyond any human power of imagination. In Catholic doctrine such divine transcendence is tempered by the taking on of human nature by the Second Person in God. The revelation of God of Himself to human beings through the Incarnation made it possible for the Christian mystics to know that what is self-evidently good in human beings is a true reflection of God.

William Blake epitomized the non-Christian conventional mystic wisdom: "For Mercy, Pity, Peace and Love/Is God our Father dear/And Mercy, Pity, Peace and Love/Is man, His child and care." Without the Incarnation his verses would not be so true in view of famine, pestilence, war, and death.

Every official liturgical prayer of the Church is addressed to God the Father, but always *through* Christ, our Lord Jesus. *Through* means that we have prayed to Jesus first and with Him offered our prayer to the Father. Not to use the Way ("I am the Way," Jesus said) is to detour from the path to God.

CHAPTER TWO

JESUS

*Questions on why Jesus called Himself
the Son of Man,
accepting Jesus as Savior,
where the name Christ came from, and more.*

Jesus

Q. 5. Why did Jesus call Himself the Son of Man?

A. He didn't openly. Our Lord was at some pains to conceal His divinity until the last stage of His ministry. Any open proclamation would have excited opposition to Him before He had completed training His Apostles and disciples. In His early ministry He didn't use "Son of God" or "Messiah" of Himself because doing so might bring about His immediate trial. He did use "Son of Man" in reference to Himself because the average Jew of His time did not regard that title as a claim to be the Messiah. But His disciples and Zacchaeus could have understood it that way.

Son of Man was used about a hundred times in seven books of the Jewish Scriptures but never as a specific title for the Messiah. In Hebrew it was *ben adam,* which can be translated *Son of Man* or *Son of Adam,* since *Adam* is the name of the first man and *adam* (without a capital letter *A*) means all his descendants.

Our Lord spoke in Aramaic, not Hebrew, and most of those who listened, I suppose, took it that He was using an idiom of that language. *Son of Man* to them could have meant just "I" or "me." As you know, the same event or the same saying of our Lord is often included by more than one of the Gospel writers who tell the same story or event in different words. In the Beatitudes as given by Matthew (chapter 5) Jesus says "Blessed are you when men revile you . . . on account of me." In Luke he says "Blessed are you when men . . . revile you . . . on account of the Son of Man."

There are many other instances in our Lord's speech when there seems to be no reason for using any title for Himself. "I" or "me" would serve just as well. The explanation that He was using an idiom of his Aramaic language seems likely enough. Most languages have similar expressions to avoid using "I" for one reason or another. "Here's a man who will not vote that way" means "I will not vote that way" and so on. There is also the circumstance that while Christ uses the title *Son of Man* to mean Himself so often, other persons in the Gospels never use it as his title. One would think they would, if Jesus Himself was using it to indicate more than "I" or "me."

There have been literally hundreds of books written on the subject and not all of them are satisfied with saying that the title was just an idiom of the Lord's language.

When you look at the Gospels more closely you can see that there were times when He used *Son of Man* as more than a substitute for "I" or "me." He uses it when He is telling about his future coming in judgment, when He is talking about establishing the

Kingdom of God, and especially when He is speaking of the suffering He will endure in His Passion. These were actions only of the expected Messiah.

Our conclusion must be that our Lord took an expression from the Scriptures and made a Messianic title of it. By using it He was proclaiming Himself the Messiah but not to everybody all at once. Those close to Him were brought gradually to a complete understanding of who He was and what He was claiming for Himself. His enemies could be left to think He was only using a synonym for "I" or "me."

The Lord's plan did not include any early revelation of His Messiahship, lest, as we saw, He be brought to trial too early. There was also the danger that popular enthusiasm might interfere with His work of training and teaching. At least once He hid from the populace so that they would not force Him to be their king.

This running away might seem to be a denial that He was entitled to be called a king, just as calling Himself *Son of Man* might seem to be a denial that He was the Son of God. But when the time came, He openly claimed kingship in the face of Pilate. Just before being hauled before Pilate He used *Son of Man* to say He would be seated at the right hand of the power of God. His enemies asked if that meant He was the Son of God, and He used the same idiom He would use in answering Pilate's question about being a king, "You say that I am." This was the most solemn form of affirmation in His language. We have an approximation of it in American slang, "You said it," meaning, "You have spoken the absolute truth." So the Lord at the time of His Passion was using the titles *Son of Man* and *Son of God* as equivalents.

He tells the high priest ". . . you will see the Son of Man seated at the right hand of the Power and coming on the clouds of heaven." Now, it is obvious that He was speaking of Himself. What is not so obvious is the reference to Daniel's vision of the Ancient of Days (God) before whom "with the clouds of heaven there came One like a Son of Man . . . And to Him was given dominion and glory and kingdom, that all peoples, nations and languages should serve Him; His dominion is an everlasting dominion which shall not pass away . . ."

"Clouds of heaven" is the key expression. In the utterances and visions of the prophets, God was seen as appearing "with the clouds of heaven." And, of course, He spoke out of a cloud to Moses in giving him the Ten Commandments, and in the desert went before the wandering Israelites as a pillar of cloud. Christ, by using the expression *clouds of heaven* while speaking of Himself, claimed divinity and made a prophecy out of Daniel's vision of the Ancient of Days and one like a "son of man." By calling Himself the "Son of Man," He was claiming "everlasting dominion which shall not pass away." To all understanding Jews, of course, such a dominion could be only that of the Messiah.

There are other reasons why He used it. When you stop to think of it, those who witnessed His miracles and His risen life might rather logically come to the conclusion that He was not a man at all but God who had taken on the outward appearance of a man as the angels did from time to time. As a matter of fact there was a heresy in the very early Church to exactly that effect. By using *Son of Man* of Himself habitually, Christ taught that He was *ben adam,* son of man, a member of mankind, one of us, not just a mythical visiting god like the pagans believed of some of their deities.

He reinforced this teaching every time He used *Son of Man* of Himself when predicting His Passion and identifying Himself with the Suffering Servant of God written about by the prophet Isaiah. After the Transfiguration He asked "... how is it that it is written of the Son of Man that He should suffer many things and be treated with contempt?" Peter, James, and John after that experience might well forget that He was anything but God, but the Lord reminded them of His humanity, along with the warning not to speak yet of this vision they had.

A final reason for our Lord's use of the term *Son of Man* was surely to teach His followers that His life and sacrifice was for all humanity. He was not just a son of David or Abraham but of Adam, from whom the whole human race sprang. He was a member of that race and for that race He lived and died.

Q. 6. Are we to believe that Jesus as a child had to learn His ABC's like other children? Since He was God as well as man wasn't He born knowing all things?

A. Yes, but things like the ABC's were *learned* as part of what is called His "experimental knowledge." The Epistle to the Hebrews says He "*learned* obedience through what He suffered." Christ knew what obedience was, but He added practical human experience to the theoretical knowledge He already had. Another name for His theoretical knowledge is "infused knowledge." Christ had knowledge of things like matrix algebra, propositional calculus, and atomic physics, but not the experience of using it. Had the occasion arisen His human mind could have invented the music of Bach, the mathematics of Einstein, or the artificial intelligence of the computer. In addition to experimental and theoretical (infused) knowledge, He had the Beatific Vision of God, the supreme knowledge which other men and women can attain only after death.

How and on exactly what these various kinds of knowledge operated will remain forever mysterious to us. We can say that His teaching in the Temple at the age of twelve was merely the action of a bright boy, but such claims as His "I and the Father are one" are not the result of any human knowledge. Modernistic Christian theologians who preach such things as that Christ did not know He was the Messiah until His baptism by John, do not begin with the belief that He was God and had the Beatific Vision from the instance of His human conception. It is true that in His ordinary actions there was nothing to indicate His possession of divine knowledge. But we know it was there from His extraordinary actions, such as the predictions of the manner of His death and His resurrection.

Q. 7. What is this business about accepting Jesus as our Savior and inviting Him into our hearts so that He will change our lives? How do we know when we have accepted Jesus as our Savior?

A. Part of your puzzlement comes from the metaphorical or poetic term "Jesus in my heart." It can mean different things to different people. A little child would say that Jesus was in his heart after receiving Holy Communion. A devout Protestant might mean that he *felt* the presence of the Savior himself. An atheistic scientist might tell you that your heart is a pump for your blood and that he doesn't know how an historical personage could be there. A Catholic theologian's first question to you would be to ask if you meant being in "the state of grace." In the Catholic sacramental system, the presence of sanctifying grace is the same as the presence of Jesus. You can determine whether you are in the state of grace by asking yourself whether you are baptized, and have confessed, repented, and received absolution for all your mortal sins. If you can say Yes to all this you have Jesus in your heart, no matter how you feel—elated or depressed.

Certain forms of Protestantism reject this part of the sacramental system of the Catholic Church and would seem to make your feelings of certainty in the matter the only way of knowing whether Jesus is in your heart. "Accepting Jesus as your Savior" is another expression from Protestant devotional theology. The Catholic equivalent is Baptism and the renewal of baptismal vows upon reaching the age of reason, together with the sincere recital of an act of faith or one of the accepted creeds. This will give a Catholic the certainty of having accepted Jesus as Savior.

Q. 8. What are we to make of statements in the Bible that say you cannot be saved unless you believe in Christ? Does this mean that millions of Moslims, Hindus, Buddhists, and pagans are condemned to hell?

A. It may sound ridiculously rigorous to say so, but the first thing you must consider is that God does not owe salvation (heaven, eternal bliss, participation in his nature) to anyone. No human being can "earn" salvation. It is a gift.

Note also that believing and being baptized do not guarantee salvation but only make it possible. The human person, a creature of God, was given a knowledge of right and wrong and consequently has an obligation to obey God whether that brings a reward or not.

Since God is infinitely just, non-Christians who obey Him through their natural sense of right and wrong will not be "condemned to everlasting punishment" but neither will they by the fact of merely existing be entitled to participate in the nature of God. Belief and Baptism will bring that entitlement to Christians.

But God is infinitely merciful as well as infinitely

just, which accounts for the Vatican Council II statement (in *Lumen Gentium*):

> Eternal salvation is open to those who, through no fault of their own, do not know Christ and His Church but seek God with a sincere heart, and under the inspiration of their conscience. Nor does Divine Providence deny the aids necessary for salvation to those who, without blame on their part, have not yet reached an explicit belief in God, but strive to lead a good life, under the influence of God's grace.

The Bible *does* say all this but not in one specific statement or text. It is dangerous to conclude from any single text that heaven is closed to any person, since it was Christ's desire that all men (and women) be saved. Those who are to be condemned are those who were given the grace to believe but refused it.

Q. 9. Where did the name Christ come from?

A. We have to start with really ancient times in the Holy Land. People in that hot, dry climate were accustomed to rub themselves with olive oil after bathing, and it was part of standard hospitality to offer this amenity to a guest. Oil was also used medicinally (balm) and in civil-religious ceremonies like the enthronement of the king.

The king thus became an "anointed one." The Hebrew word for this was *messiah* and eventually the great king who was to restore Israel came to be called *the* Messiah. Peter recognized Jesus as *the* Messiah (Matthew, chapter 16, verse 13). In Greek, which like Hebrew had a word for *the,* this title was *o Christos, the* Christ.

The Apostles and disciples preached about *the* Christ. Their listeners, perhaps confused by the accents of the strangers, often mistook *Christos* for *chrestos* which meant only "good man." This mistake made it seem to them that the new doctrine was just a moral philosophy about being good instead of a teaching based on historical reality. So bearers of the Gospel began to use *Christ* as a name, dropping the *the,* indicating that Jesus was a real person and not just an imaginary ideal man. St. Paul sometimes uses *Christ* alone as the Savior's name, sometimes *Christ Jesus,* but the most frequent usage is *Jesus Christ,* which occurs in the first chapters of the Gospels of Matthew, Mark, and John as well as in the Acts of the Apostles and in the Epistle to the Romans. Latin does not have any word which would translate the Greek word *o* or the Hebrew definite article (*the* in English) so the form Jesus Christ became more prevalent than *Jesus the Christ* when anything about the Savior was translated from Latin into, for example, English.

Q. 10. Why does the birthday of Jesus remain the same each year while Good Friday, the day He died, comes on a different date each year?

A. Christmas is dated from the apparent movement of the sun, Easter and Good Friday from the apparent movements of the moon. We don't know the dates of

Christ's birth and death with complete certainty because the New Testament was written centuries before our Gregorian calendar was instituted. Many different systems of keeping track of passing time were in force then.

The winter solstice pagan feast, December 25, was adopted rather early in the history of the Church in Rome as the birthday of Christ. There is no reason to change the date of the observance, even though it is not possible now to prove that that was the exact date.

Good Friday's date depends on the date of Easter. The movement of the Easter date was established for the Roman Church only after many difficulties with the systems of datekeeping in the various parts of the world. The Council of Nicaea decided in 325 that Easter was to be celebrated on the first Sunday following the first full moon after the spring solstice (our March 21).

The moon comes into the question because the Jewish year was made up of twelve months, six of thirty days and six of twenty-nine days, each of which began with the new moon, the night when not even a sliver of the moon was to be seen. There were three official witnesses to this who spread the news with bonfire signals. This gave their year only 354 days, so every three years (or so) they had to average things out by having thirteen months. The additional month was decreed by the Sanhedrin council of Jewish elders. Any communities not in communication with the Sanhedrin had to figure out their own date for the Jewish Passover.

Christians knew when Christ's death and Resurrection happened on this Jewish calendar but didn't always agree on how to figure it out for their current year. The Fathers of Nicaea specified that Easter fall on Sunday because some systems made it fall on week days. They knew the first *full* moon would occur on the Jewish date 14th Nisan, (our March-April), which established the Jewish Passover, certainly the time of the death and resurrection of the Lord. They made the Easter date fall just after the spring solstice, March 21, because everyone could agree on when this happened. When local calendars made Easter unduly early or late in the year, the local Christian Church authorities would have an evident and sure event from which to calculate the date of Easter.

Q. 11. Why do we make so much of the suffering and death of Christ when He was spared so many of the tragedies other human beings go through?

A. Most of all because of who He was, not only the perfect Man but God incarnate. That other human beings have suffered longer or different pains is inconsequential. Another reason for "making much of" Christ's suffering is that it was accepted willingly as a substitute for the suffering that would otherwise be justly visited on sinners. No matter how intense the pain suffered by other men and women, it has no power to satisfy for sin unless it is offered in union with the suffering of Christ.

Atheistic philosophers (Camus, Sartre) to whom this Catholic concept is "irrelevant" are driven to nausea and suicide by the ills of quite ordinary human experiences, let alone such afflictions as you mention.

A third reason to marvel at the suffering of Christ is that He Himself willed it. It is human nature to avoid pain if possible and even against the moral law to harm or to kill our own bodies. Christ as Lord of all life and death was above this law, but His pain was no less intense because of that circumstance. Why He, who was omnipotent, chose His own suffering as a means of redeeming humanity, rather than something we might call a general amnesty, is part of the larger problem of all evil.

We know that humans (unlike the plants) feel pain and (unlike the animals) have moral responsibility. If we were not above the level of these lower life forms, we might experience God's goodness as they do, but we would not intellectually *know* God's goodness. Sin and suffering make us realize the difference between good and evil, i.e., the difference between the will of God and the will of creatures who use their free will in opposition to His.

The serpent in the Garden of Eden was right in promising Adam and Eve that they would *know* "good and evil," and the Easter liturgy calls Adam's sin a "happy fault," a contradiction in terms. The problem and the mystery of evil remain, but the lesson is that God is "so good" that He brings ultimate happiness to humanity in spite of its disobedience.

A final consideration in answer to your question is that since Christ was the perfect Man, His human nervous system was more sensitive than that of any other human being ever born and therefore His suffering was greater than that of any other human person. He did not escape mental pain, as we know from His bloody sweat in the Garden of Gethsemane as He faced the prospect of death by crucifixion, and from His quoting the psalmist as He hung on the cross, "My God, my God, why has thou forsaken me?"

Q. 12. What did Jesus Christ mean when He said He would sit at the "right hand of the Father" after His ascension into heaven?

A. He meant He was God. But you must consider the spiritual background to arrive at that conclusion.

In His dealings with the Jewish religious leaders, Jesus reserved this most dramatic assertion for the very end of His trial before the Sanhedrin. He had answered the accusation of the high priest that He had claimed He was the Christ, the Son of God, with the strongest possible affirmation. "You have said so," an idiom in His language with the same meaning as our modern slang, "You said it." It was then that He went on to indicate that He was God by saying He would be seen "at the right hand of the Power"— *Power* being understood by all present as meaning the one true Father God.

But what most probably caused the high priest to cry "Blasphemy!" was that He also said He would be seen "coming on the clouds of heaven." This was a reference to the vision of the Prophet Daniel, chapter 7, verse 13, of one like the Son of Man to whom was given "everlasting dominion," and who came on the clouds of heaven. Obviously, to the learned Sanhedrin this one was the expected Messiah.

The high priest understood that Jesus was laying claim to a twin throne with Daniel's "Ancient of Days" (Daniel, chapter 7, verse 9), who again to the Sanhedrin was obviously God the Father. Coming on the clouds of heaven and sitting at the right hand of the Father meant the same thing to the learned Sanhedrin. They clearly saw that Jesus was asserting that He had a part in the administration of creation. He was claiming to be God, which in their court was just what they wanted. We know what Jesus meant from their reaction. They felt entirely justified in condemning Him to death.

To sit at the right hand of any ruler has always meant being honored, probably for the primordial reason that there are more right-handed people than there are left-handed. But in the context of Daniel's vision, Jesus used the expression to proclaim His equality (twin thrones) with God the Father.

The Church uses the expression "right hand of the Father" in both the Apostles' and the Nicene Creed to affirm Christ's equality with the Father and consequent divinity.

CHAPTER THREE

THE SACRAMENTS AND THE LITURGY

*Questions on why Catholics baptize babies,
why Christians of all faiths cannot
receive Communion together,
why Catholics confess their sins to a priest,
and much more.*

The Sacraments and the Liturgy

Q. 13. Must babies still be baptized as soon as possible after birth? Or has this rule changed?

A. Canon 867 of the Code of Canon Law says that parents must see to it that infants are baptized within a few weeks after birth. Those arrangements for the Baptism are to be made as soon as possible after birth or even before birth. It further states that an infant in danger of death is to be baptized without delay. It does not say anything about unbaptized infants who die being excluded from heaven. That is a dogmatic, not a legislative matter.

Mainstream theologians have taken the words of Christ to Nicodemus, "Truly, truly, I say to you, unless one is born of water and the Spirit, he cannot enter the kingdom of God," to mean that the unbaptized are excluded. Cardinal Cajetan did not think they were, and his opinion was censured but not condemned at the Council of Trent. St. Bonaventure maintained that

43

some, if not all, such infants, went to heaven by the special mercy of God.

It is small comfort to bereaved parents of un-baptized children to reflect that heaven, even to saints, is a free gift of God and that the dead babies may be given other gifts of happiness. But they can reflect on God's infinite goodness and the possibility that He grants salvation in extraordinary ways as well as the ordinary way of Baptism in the Church.

Though it really is not, to our human minds it seems a divine injustice that a person deprived of Baptism—whether through the indifference of parents, or being aborted or miscarried, or the carelessness of the person baptizing not observing one of the essentials of the Sacrament (such as the physical washing of the body by water)—should be excluded from heaven. But neither can our human minds or laws limit the infinite mercy of God toward His human creatures, baptized or not.

The law about not delaying Baptism exists to teach the faithful that the ordinary everyday mercy of God, offering a means of salvation, should not be spurned.

Q. 14. In Baptism, can one of the godparents be Prot-estant?

A. Canon 874 of the Code of Canon Law of 1983 says that a sponsor (godparent) is to be a Catholic who has been confirmed, has made his or her First Communion, and is living as a practicing member of the Church. But it permits a member of another Church to be present as a witness of the Baptism in addition to the Catholic sponsor. In most cases this will take care of the social aspects of the ceremony, since there are no rules about proclaiming a distinction between witness and sponsor at the ceremony itself.

The Church could not ask a professing Protestant to violate his or her conscience and promise to bring up a child in a religion he or she does not believe in. At the same time, the Church could not permit the religious welfare of a Catholic child (or adult) to be sacramentally entrusted to the care of a person whose beliefs and intentions the Church has no way of ascertaining.

The law is the same for infant or adult Baptism. In the latter case it is easy to understand the historical need for a Catholic sponsor. In the early days of the Church, when most Baptisms were of adults because whole nations were being converted, one function of a sponsor was to vouch for the sincerity and suitability of the candidate for Baptism to the Christian community of which the sponsor was a member. A Christian of another faith couldn't do that any more than he or she could provide an education in the truths of the faith to the candidate.

Q. 15. Why do Catholics baptize babies since our Lord Himself wasn't baptized by John the Baptist until He was a grown man?

A. Christ did not receive the sacrament of Baptism. He received only the "baptism of John" which was not a sacrament and which is distinguished from the sacrament of the Bible (Acts 14:1-6).

Christ submitted to it to show approval of the preaching of John and to seize the occasion of making ordinary water capable of removing original sin. The "power," as we might say, went from Christ to the water instead of from the water to the person baptized as it does in the case of Christians being baptized.

With these considerations understood, there is no way of imitating our Lord in age when receiving the sacrament, since He didn't receive the sacrament at any age. Good Christians give the sacrament to babies if they are reasonably certain that the babies will eventually accept the faith because of proper upbringing and Christian parentage. Even those babies that do not have this prospect but are in danger of death should be baptized because Baptism is necessary in the ordinary sacramental process of salvation provided for us by God.

Infant Baptism is an insurance against the danger of not receiving the sacrament through early death. It is true that the more free will one brings to the reception of the sacrament, the more incidental graces are received, but these are negligible compared to the indelible mark of Baptism itself.

Q. 16. What would you say to the argument that Christ meant the Eucharist to be only a symbol of His Body and Blood and that in any event He said only "Do this

**in memory of Me" without restricting His command
to priests?**

A. The Catholic doctrine of the reality of the Body and
Blood of Christ in the Eucharist does not depend only
on what He said at the Last Supper but also on what
He said in His promise of the Eucharist in the sixth
chapter of St. John's Gospel. He drove away many of
His followers who said His saying was hard to believe.
He could easily have recalled them by saying that His
"flesh to eat" and His "blood to drink" were only
symbolic statements, but He did not. He let them go
away when they would not accept His statements
literally.

As for the priesthood being necessary to confect the
Eucharist, Christ spoke the words of commission, "Do
this in memory of Me," only to a carefully selected,
very small group of His followers called His Apostles.
He did not tell the crowds that followed Him to have
picnic suppers in His memory. But points like this are
only school-debate arguments.

To understand the Eucharist and the Real Presence
you really should know something about the history
of religion, the place of sacrifice in it, and why other
sacrifices are worthless in comparison with the Body
and Blood of the God-Man. This will lead you into the
doctrine of the Trinity which in turn will demonstrate
the need and logic of many other doctrines. The
Catholic faith is like a pattern on a Persian rug or on a
tapestry. Once you see how a doctrine fits into a

pattern you can see its necessity. If you just cut off a corner of the tapestry and look only at it, you won't see much of anything.

Q. 17. In explaining the Eucharist to those outside the Catholic Church, 1. how can we believe that bread and wine is changed into the Body and Blood of Christ? And 2. if we do believe, aren't we eating human flesh, which is something only cannibals do?

A. 1. We believe in the change because of the words of Christ at the Last Supper and His promise of the Eucharist some time before the Last Supper. 2. We feel no revulsion in eating human flesh and blood because the apparent food (bread and wine) does not have the taste, etc., of flesh and blood; because we are not eating it primarily to fulfill our physical need for physical food; because from the most ancient times known to humanity eating the victim was part of any sacrifice to the deity, and the Mass is a sacrifice; because this physical union of our bodies with the Body of Christ symbolizes the union between God and humanity that occurred when Christ took on a human nature and which will be made permanent when we believers participate in the divine nature in heaven. This little list by no means exhausts the reasons why we don't feel like cannibals, but it should be long enough to furnish food for thought.

Incidentally, the charge of cannibalism against partakers of the Eucharist is almost as old as the Eucharist. The pagans hearing only second- and third-hand versions of what went on in the Christian assemblies often concluded that it was cannibalism in literal fact. Athenagoras, an Athenian philosopher and convert to Christianity in the second century, defended his Church. After accepting this delusion on the part of the pagans as a fact of life, he explained the Christian concern for life, the Christian opposition to the pagan custom of abortion of unwanted children. He argued that Christians could not really be killing and eating babies in their secret Eucharists since they had reverence for life, temporal and eternal.

Q. 18. Do Catholics believe it is the timeless, risen Jesus who is present in the Host, or the historical, human Jesus who lived two thousand years ago?

A. Both. All the adjectives you apply to Jesus—*timeless, risen, historical, human*—are true of the single person Jesus. I am no expert on Protestant theologies, but many other Christian Churches seem to believe in the temporary presence of the "timeless, risen" Jesus because those words suggest only a spiritual reality. They seem to have the same difficulty some of the Jews and some of the disciples had in accepting the Lord's words when He promised them His human flesh to eat and His human blood to drink.

Admittedly, the doctrine and the manner of His presence are mysterious, but the Catholic Church insists on the real human presence of Christ in the Eucharist, body, blood, and soul, as well as divinity.

Although Christ never specifically commanded it,

Catholics adore the Sacred Species, and many Eucharistic devotions have arisen because of the Catholic belief that Christ continues His real human presence in the consecrated bread and wine from the moment of consecration to the time when the appearances of bread and wine cease to exist.

Christ spoke the words of institution before giving the bread to His Apostles, not while they were eating it, so His presence did not depend on the physical act of eating in common, as some have falsely taught.

Although the word *transubstantiation* does not occur frequently in the post-Vatican II Church, the doctrine that only the substance of the bread is changed into the substance of Christ's Body accounts for the fact that one cannot *see* the Body of Christ. But it also brings the logical necessity of a continuing presence because substances continue in existence until someone changes them. Christ never said anything about changing His Body and Blood back to ordinary bread and wine as it would be necessary to hold in the "temporary presence" theologies.

Q. 19. Did the early Church use both bread and wine? When did the Church stop offering the cup to the laity? Why has the Church now decided to offer both at Mass? Finally, does the Church regard the Bread and Wine used in Protestant services as something to be regarded as sacred?

A. Communion was under the form of both bread and wine down to the twelfth century for public occasions. Communion was carried under the form of bread alone to the sick. Children below the age of reason were given only the consecrated wine and at other times were given only the unconsumed consecrated bread left over from the public ceremony. (The idea was that they were innocent of sin and therefore suitable receptacles.) There was no divine precept that made both species necessary for all.

No one had any thought but that lay Communion was valid under either species alone, so eventually the greater convenience of using only the bread made that practice universal. The Council of Trent (1545-1563) decreed that Mass was not valid without the priest consuming both species, but that the laity were not to be given the cup, even though a few theologians argued that more grace was received when communicating under both kinds.

The Tridentine decrees destroyed part of the symbolism of spiritual sustenance. That is to say, the need human beings have of both food and drink for physical life symbolized the Christian need of both Body and Blood (bread and wine) for spiritual life. But the Council of Trent issued its decrees anyway because certain thinkers were falsely insisting that there was a divine precept for the use of both bread and wine, and that the Church was sacrilegious in limiting the laity to one species.

The answer to your question about why the Church has now made exceptions to these decrees of Trent is that the legislators saw the force of the symbolism and thought it would increase the piety of the laity. But they made the use of the cup optional because there are about as many persons passively against the use of the cup for hygienic reasons as there are persons positively advocating its use for symbolic reasons.

As for your final point, the Catholic Church regards the Communion services of the Protestants as beautiful acts of worship of the true God performed by persons bearing the name Christian, but has to agree with most of them that the bread and wine *they* use in worship are not the Body and Blood of Christ, at most they symbolize them.

Q. 20. Why is it that thieves, murderers, child molesters, and others who break God's law can receive the Eucharist, but the divorced person or someone married to a divorced person is denied Holy Communion?

A. In your list of malefactors you must include the word *repentant*. Also, before any explanation is begun, it must be understood that divorce by itself does not necessarily bar anyone from Communion. It is remarriage without annulment of the first marriage that invokes the penalty.

In the present social and religious upheaval, divorces are becoming almost as numerous as marriages. The Church marriage laws that once seemed right and reasonable to most persons of good will now affect the lives of Catholics who can't always see how the law is being fair to them.

The catch is, of course, that anyone entering on a remarriage unblessed by the Church is entering into a perduring state of disobedience to that Church. The other sinners you mentioned can repent, confess, and return to Communion. The invalidly married person cannot give up the sin without giving up the marriage, which often (when children are involved) seems morally impossible.

But the Church cannot admit to Communion those in invalid marriages without utterly destroying the teaching that sacramental marriage is one of the channels of grace established by Christ. The Church was given authority by Christ to determine which marriages are channels of grace and which are not. The dilemma for the invalidly married is that no matter how good their intentions are they cannot obey and disobey at the same time.

The Church is trying to meet the crisis by examining first-marriage contracts more carefully and granting annulments when they are found not to be, let us say, of sacramental quality. It is requiring expressed comprehension of the meaning of the sacramental contract, rather than assuming it or accepting a perfunctory written promise about observing Christian marriage essentials. It is educating Catholics about the seriousness of the Catholic marriage contract.

But what it cannot do is call disobedience obedience or abdicate the authority and responsibility given it by God. The ultimate consolation of those in unabandonable invalid marriages is that Holy Communion is not necessary for salvation, and that the public penance endured by exclusion from Communion will not be overlooked in the judgment of God.

Q. 21. Why shouldn't all Christians be allowed and encouraged to take part in the Eucharist? Wouldn't this be a giant step toward Christian unity?

A. "Christian unity" needs an exact definition. As it stands it can mean doctrinal, disciplinary, or political agreement. Calling on everybody to take Communion could possibly benefit some kind of political unity, but certainly would not lead to doctrinal or disciplinary unity.

As a matter of fact, all truly ecumenical organizations begin with the understanding that they are not in business to change anyone's beliefs. Their purpose is to promote "dialogue," leading to understanding of the attitudes of other Christians and to the elimination of misunderstandings which in the past have been serious enough to lead to hatred and open war.

Another consideration is that the Eucharist in Catholic theology is not a means toward any other end. It is itself the final and supreme act of worship, the union of human beings with Christ in the perfect and all-sufficient sacrifice of Himself for our sakes. It takes considerable study and good will to come to that knowledge and belief. To participate in the Eucharist merely physically and not with full spiritual understanding is not really a rational act.

Again, terms need definition. For certain Protestants whose belief is that the Eucharist is only a symbol of unity, and without other meaning, the act of participation within their own denomination can be rational. But the doctrinal Eucharistic unity of Christendom has been broken through the centuries by denominations which do not accept the doctrines which obtained when that Eucharistic unity prevailed.

Q. 22. Why can't we just confess our sins and pray for forgiveness directly to God? Why do we have to confess them to a priest?

A. The Church's argument is not only that Christ gave the power of forgiving and not forgiving sins to His Apostles (Gospel of John, chapter 20, verse 23) but that He was following elementary human psychology in granting this power. There is a deep need in the rational human person who has sinned to have an outward sign of forgiveness. If everyone could just forgive himself after a confession to God, human psychology being what it is, some people would grow into sinful ways even though they admitted the ways were sinful. And really no one could be sure of forgiveness, since God seldom gives direct signs to individuals and since only the individual could be judge of the sign anyway. A spoken formula of absolution, given by a person delegated by God through the Church to grant such absolutions, who knows what the sins were and who has the special education to judge the malice of the sins, can give a certainty of reconciliation with God that no amount of private prayer can achieve.

The Church's Sacrament of Reconciliation, as Confession is now called, has rituals which emphasize this aspect of outward reconciliation. The idea is that the penitent is reconciled to the Christian community and that the community, by its acceptance of him as a member, rejoices in the outward sign of absolution given by the priest. The Christian community is thus composed of persons who can be sure that other persons in the community all have the same standards of morality, that they have opened their consciences to judgment. The Christian community is not made up of persons varying in their standards of morality, keeping their own counsel about their own guilt or innocence, and allowing no other judgment to be made. So confessing your sins to a priest is sort of your membership card in the Christian community. It means that the community recognizes you as a member and it is your ticket of admission.

Q. 23. The Pope has urged frequent use of the Sacrament of Reconciliation in an apostolic exhortation. But how do we make a good "confession of devotion" when we are not confessing mortal sins? Repetition of the same venial sins can be very monotonous.

A. Attend parish penance services which include the spoken confession of sins to a confessor. You do not have to go back to recitations by rote that may have been your custom in the past. Venial sins can be confessed generically or even with the statement "I have sinned venially." If you are afraid that this will annoy the confessor by infringing on his time, remember that the Pope's exhortation was addressed to priests as well as laity, and that unless they willingly share the physical and mental burdens involved in celebrating the sacrament, its use will decline in spite of anything the Pope says.

The Pope repeated that group confession and general absolution may be used only in cases of grave necessity. The "sense of sin" has pretty well been eliminated in our secular culture. It has been maintained in the Catholic Church chiefly by the requirement of individual confession of individual sins. If too many members of the Church lose the sense of sin, God will be greatly dishonored.

The Christian faith begins with a Creator who gave free will to some of His creatures. Ideally the free will of men and women coincides with the will of God. Practically (and even perhaps metaphysically) the existence of more than one free will ends (as we know from Adam's sin) in a difference between them. Confession and ritual absolution of the differences human beings cause is the only way of getting back to the ideal.

Union of God's will and our will is another way of saying "heaven." So even if you have only venial sins, and even though confessing them is monotonous, repetitious, and boring to all concerned, the thought that you are trying to unite your will with God's here on earth so that the union can be continued in heaven should make frequent confession a part of your life.

Q. 24. I hear that there are now penitential services where the priest absolves everybody without private confession. Has this been approved by the Pope?

A. Only conditionally. The conditions are 1. anyone getting absolved from mortal sin must go to confession in the usual way later and before getting general absolution again for further mortal sin. 2. Mortal sinners must confess at least once a year in the regular way despite any general absolutions. 3. General absolution can be given only when there is no time for the usual hearing of confessions (soldiers going into battle, for instance). 4. There must be a real lack of priests. If there are enough available priests to hear the confessions, general absolution cannot be given. It does not matter how many persons there are who wish absolution.

It goes without saying that examination of conscience, sorrow for sin, acceptance of penance, and resolution not to sin again are still required for sacramental forgiveness of sin. Some people mistakenly think that general absolution without oral and auricular confession of sins would be a good thing to have all the time, that it would make life easier and attract people to the Church. But those who think like that forget that there are just as many persons who need that assurance of forgiveness which comes only when the sin has been told to, and understood by, a priest who has been given the power by Christ to forgive.

Many normal people, not only neurotics, get no sense of forgiveness from solitary consideration of their own sins or from any decision of their own that Almighty God has pardoned them. Confession plus absolution removes the "guilt feelings" the psychiatrists talk about, as well as the guilt before God in the case of normal rational people who have sinned and vocally repented. Such people feel somehow cheated when told that their unconfessed sins have been taken away. They feel that way not because they want to keep the sins but because sincere repentance makes them want to suffer punishment for them, at least the indignity of admitting them to someone other than themselves.

Q. 25. What if I go to confession and receive absolution from a priest who is not in good standing with the Church?

A. As long as the penitent has no sins to confess that would be considered non-sins by such a priest *and* as long as the priest has "faculties" (permission or appointment by the local bishop to hear confessions) the penitent need not worry at all about the validity of the absolution. The Church has put the burden of determining the worthiness of a priest to hear confessions upon the bishop, not on the penitents who approach the priest.

But a penitent with self-known sins going on purpose to a priest who didn't think the penitent was sinful would be like a person trying to lose weight by changing the numbers on the scale. He can't fool himself.

One of the mistaken teachings of the ancient Donatist heresy was that sacraments administered by a priest in mortal sin were invalid and did the recipient no spiritual good. But if these Donatist teachings were true, nobody could ever be sure of receiving any sacrament since nobody can ever be sure of a particular priest's state of sin or non-sin.

If you confess what you consider your sins to a priest who has the "faculties of the diocese" (that ordinarily means any priest hearing confessions at announced times in a Catholic Church), you need not worry about the validity of the absolution. Even if something is irregular in such a priest's position, there is another theological principle known as *Ecclesia supplet*, which means that the Church judges the penitent innocent of wrongdoing and the spiritual effect on him the same as a valid absolution.

Q. 26. I was told growing up Catholic that no priest had ever revealed anything he had ever heard in confession, no matter what his character. Is this true?

A. First, to prove it true, even to yourself, you would have to have perfect knowledge of every act in the life of every priest who ever heard a confession. Practically speaking it is impossible to prove a universal negative.

Another reason for not believing that the seal of confession has been perfectly observed is that the Church has always had laws about it and specified penalties for priests who break the seal, which would be absurd if there were never any cases of its being broken. The seal of confession has been sensationalized in Gothic novels about the days when kings and queens had private confessors who advised them in civil as well as moral matters and who received information about kingly political plans and intentions at the same time.

In real life, what is told in confession is pretty drab and from one penitent to the next repetitive to the point of boredom. Nearly all civilized states have laws protecting the confessor in his obligation of secrecy, but in the rare cases where a confessor might in some way benefit by "revealing" sins, who would believe he was telling the truth? Most codes of civil law forbid the introduction of evidence received in confession, not only to protect the confessor, but also to protect the court from testimony offered by a person admitting sacrilege by the very act of testifying.

Q. 27. Why do Catholics have the custom of anointing the sick? What prayers are used?

A. The Church has an official Ritual with the specified prayers for all the sacraments and has special prayers and a ritual of anointing for what is now called the "Anointing of the Sick." Only a priest (Canon 1003) can administer the actual sacrament, although there is certainly no prohibition of anyone saying prayers in medical emergencies.

The sacrament (from about 1100 to 1983) used to be unofficially called Extreme Unction, a name that had overtones of the last moments of life on earth. Though the Church never taught that the sacrament was necessary for salvation, popular piety correctly insisted that the sacrament be received by the dying whenever possible. That is still the attitude of the Church. The idea that a person had to be at the point of death before receiving the sacrament is now overruled by Canon 1002. It provides for the anointing in groups of persons who may be only "sick" or suffering the infirmities of old age.

In scheduled communal anointings the emphasis, so to speak, is now on "healing" rather than on receiving a "final" (extreme) sacrament just before departing this life.

The Catholic Church is the only Christian Church which regards the Anointing of the Sick as a real sacrament. It does so because when our Lord first sent His Apostles, (the Twleve) they "anointed with oil many that were sick and healed them" (Mark, chapter 6, verse 13). And, of course, there is the recommendation and the promise of James In his Epistle: "Is any among you sick? Let him call for the elders of the Church and let them pray over him, anointing him with oil in the name of the Lord and the prayer of faith will save the sick man, and the Lord will raise him up and if he has committed sins they will be forgiven."

Q. 28. If a priest wasn't available through illness or the priest shortage, could a deacon or Eucharistic minister say Mass?

A. No. The Sacrifice of the Mass can be offered only by a priest according to the most ancient traditions and legislation of the Church. The latest pronouncement on the subject from the Congregation for the Doctrine of the Faith dates from August 6, 1983. It was occasioned by the teachings of the dissident theologians Schillebeeckx and Kung and said that their reasoning "undermines the entire apostolic structure of the Church and distorts the sacramental economy of salvation itself."

By permission of the bishop, of course, a deacon or Eucharistic lay minister can conduct a Communion and prayer service, and a deacon can preach. But this is not, and must not be called, Mass or Divine Liturgy. Canon 767 allows a lay person to speak at such a gathering since it is not a Mass. At Mass only a priest or deacon may preach. This procedure is common in parts of Latin America, Africa, and Asia where priests are not available every week for Sunday Mass.

The obligation to hear Mass on Sunday does not hold for Catholics who have no priests, but it also goes without saying that the absence of the Sacrifice is greatly detrimental to the spiritual welfare of such Catholics. When they receive Communion at a prayer service they should remember that this is not the perfect worship of God, which the Mass is.

Q. 29. After the Consecration at Mass, why do we ask God the Father to "look with favor on these offerings and accept them"? Was not the sacrifice of Jesus fully acceptable to the Father?

A. Yes, and you are finding the same difficulty that all people who try to understand what they are saying or doing have encountered in this lovely passage from the First Eucharistic Prayer (Roman Canon). The solution comes in understanding what is meant by "these offerings." Ideally, we offer not only Christ but also ourselves in sacrifice. While, as you say, there is no imperfection to be corrected in the offering of Christ, when we put ourselves on the altar we cannot be sure that God will accept us, and consequently we ask for His favor.

The doctrine of the Mystical Body of Christ is involved. It is the Church—which includes Christ and ourselves—which is offered. To go on we must consider: 1. that no sacrifice of our own without Christ would bring redemption; and 2. that if we are not part of the sacrifice, the free will God gave us is not necessarily turning us back to God. If we are being redeemed only by God's fiat, the Incarnation and Passion of Christ become pointless and meaningless.

All commentaries on the Roman Canon address the difficulty you found; but they can blame no one for the lack of clarity, because the origins of the text are lost in the mists of history. Note, though, that the composers of our present Third Eucharistic Prayer saw the difficulty and made their canon read "Look with favor on your Church's offering," echoing but clarifying "Look with favor on these offerings."

Q. 30. When a Communion Host is dropped accidentally during the people's Communion at Mass, what is the proper procedure? The same reverence as of old doesn't seem to be shown to it. Why not?

A. If reverence is not shown, it is in disobedience to all the special instructions that were issued in connection with the permission to give Communion in the hand in 1977. Before the Mass was allowed to be said in English or lay ministers were permitted, the official Roman Missal contained instructions for the priest which covered the accidental dropping of a Host. It was to be reverently picked up, water was to be poured on the spot, and the surface dried with a small finger towel which was later washed and the water poured into the sacrarium. The sacrarium is a sink used only for such disposal. It leads to clean ground, not to a sewer or septic tank. This was for cases where the Host dropped to the floor. (If it fell on clothing, the procedure was not called for). The new English missals do not have such instructions.

The liturgical reformers omitted the ceremony, not because they thought that less reverence should be shown the Eucharist but because they thought that such extreme care somehow detracted from the basic symbolism according to which the Eucharist should be treated as food. That is to say, since we would not "purify" a spot where ordinary bread was dropped, we should not purify the spot where the Eucharistic Bread was dropped.

There is room for argument about that and there are still priests who "purify" out of private devotion, but such reverence is no longer included in the official missal instructions. With the introduction of lay distribution of the sacrament, instruction and catechesis of Eucharistic ministers enjoined only "reverence" in such situations. If you witness any carelessness or irreverence in the distribution of Communion, it is a case of the catechesis failing, not of any change in Church doctrine.

The old instruction left little to common sense. They provided for such things as the priest becoming nauseated and vomiting after Communion, and for poison being discovered in the chalice. But they did specify that a dropped or contaminated Host should be dissolved in a special little cup of water before being consigned to the sacrarium. That is still a good idea.

Q. 31. What was the meaning of the little bells that used to be rung at Mass, and why have they been dropped? I miss them.

A. Me too. There never was anything so devotional as the hush that used to come over the congregation at the consecration during the Mass, interrupted only by the tinkle of the bell which seemed to join in the general adoration.

Of course, all you and I remember is the custom in the English-speaking Church in our own lifetimes. In medieval England the Sanctus bell was hung outside the church and rung at the consecration for the benefit of the workers in the fields who could not come to the Mass. You can still find Sanctus bells hanging from the outside wall of old churches in England. In some of the more exotic rites within the Christian Church long ago, great gongs were used, requiring muscular young men, struck at the solemn moments of the Mass. Even I can remember learning as an altar boy just how to strike the triple-toned small gong used at Mass. The bell was largely a matter of local and historical custom, no great all-binding law was ever enacted about the bell.

As for what happened to it, I can only guess that priests and congregations in the throes of liturgical reform decided that it was only an unnecessary reminder of the time of consecration—a reminder dating from the time when people read May devotions, said the Rosary, or indulged in other purely private devotions at Mass. They should have been following the action and prayers, which was difficult to do when the prayers were in Latin.

Once the liturgical reformers brought everyone into minute-by-minute participation, there was to be no need for any special signals at the time of consecration. It's all very logical but I regret the silencing of the bells as much as you, perhaps only from sentimental reasons.

Q. 32. When did the Liturgy of the Hours or Divine Office start?

A. With the Jewish Temple observances. The name in English "Liturgy of the Hours" shows that the Church's intention is to sanctify the various parts of the day with prayer, just as the Jews did in the Temple.

Many Psalms, which are the basic fabric of the Office, refer to the time of day at which they were liturgically recited; "I will meditate on Thee in the morning," "Evening and morning and at noon I will speak and declare," "Seven times a day I have given praise to Thee."

The Christians of Apostolic times did not resign from the Jewish faith, they properly regarded their new beliefs as the flowering of the old ones they were born in. Accordingly, they attended the Temple services. Even when Christianity spread beyond the confines of the Jewish nation, they continued using the prayer forms of Judaism: recital of the Psalms and readings from the Scriptures. In time, of course, they made Christian additions. These included the letters of the Apostles, readings from the Gospels which preserved the story of the Messiah, and newly composed or extemporaneous prayers suitable to the time of the year they were being said.

We still have this sacred material as the first part of the Mass in preparation for the Eucharistic prayer. Mass, in those early times, was not offered every day. But apparently set forms of prayer were said by the

Christians every day, and the Divine Office grew out of this custom. The prayers were not the same everywhere, but by the fifth century there was considerable unity. After Pope Gregory the Great the formulas used at Rome began to predominate. It was in honor of this Pope, of course, that the music still used in the ideal recitation of the Office was named Gregorian chant. The other name for the priests' Office is the *Breviary,* a portable form of the earlier long forms—some of which were designed to last all night as vigils, preparations for the greater feasts.

CHAPTER FOUR

THE BIBLE

*Questions on who wrote the Bible,
who is the Antichrist,
how you can furnish Biblical proofs
of Catholic doctrines,
and much more.*

The Bible

Q. 33. Who wrote the Bible? And how did it come down to us?

A. Here is a summary of how the Bible came to us. First of all, we have absolutely none of the original manuscripts. Their disappearance is easy to understand in the case of the Old Testament texts, what with their antiquity, the destruction of Jerusalem, and the dispersal of the Jewish race.

In the case of the New Testament, the originals were probably worn out by constant use or destroyed in the persecutions the Church suffered in the early centuries. We have only rather inaccurate copies of inaccurate copies.

In the first two centuries when the New Testament was being copied, the writing materials were reeds or quills and sheets of papyrus. The papyrus was a plant with pith in its stem that could be cut into strips and dried. The strips were laid down vertically side by side with a horizontal layer placed on the top and the whole arrangement gummed together and sandpapered. (They used oyster shells in case you noticed an anachronism). The work usually resulted in sheets of about ten by five inches which didn't wear too well. The sheets could be glued together into strips which could be rolled up. St. Paul's Epistle to the Romans would be about twelve feet long and the Gospel of Matthew about thirty feet.

About the year 300 it became common to put the sheets into book, or codex, form. Maybe some of these codices had covers to protect them, as modern books have, and in that case the answer to your question would be "about A.D. 300." But these early collections seldom or never contained the whole Bible. The "canon," or list of truly inspired books, was still being determined. About the same time there was a general change from papyrus to parchment. Only about the year A.D. 800 were copyists able to import a kind of paper from Asia.

Fewer than twenty papyrus rolls or codices containing parts of the New Testament, and only about four thousand parchment or paper copies made before the days of printing, still exist. Nearly half of these are lectionaries which have only those parts of the New Testament that were read in the liturgy. All of these have many copyist and editorial mistakes. Also, it was the custom—pretty certain in the case of St. Paul—for authors to dictate their works to people skilled in writing. Errors could be introduced by a careless stenographer. The true original was in spoken, not written form. Scholars say that only one-tenth of 1 percent of the writing errors would make any change in the meaning. Yet the sorting of the oldest and therefore presumably the most correct manuscripts has kept scholars busy in digging out the text closest to the utterance of the scriptural authors.

The scarcity and incompleteness of manuscripts—in addition to stenographic transpositions—made it very hard to "look up" anything in the Bible. Until the thirteenth century the books of the Bible were not even divided into chapters. The Archbishop of Canterbury, Stephen Langton, did that for the Latin Vulgate version of the Bible. The further convenience of a division into verses did not come until after the invention of printing. A Dominican monk first attempted that in the early sixteenth century.

Neither the chapter nor the verse divisions were always made according to the thought of the authors, and our newest versions of the Scriptures are still trying to correct the faults, with some success. The first divisions into chapter and verse were universally accepted and now—in the face of changes—one has to stop and think which Psalm is meant when Psalm 100 is mentioned. Is it the one that used to be 99 or the one that used to be 101? However, the new Protestant and Catholic versions now agree pretty well in their corrections of the old numbers.

"Chapter-and-verse" quotation of the Scriptures became in more modern times the stock in trade of apologists and proselytizers alike. It could have been Mark Twain who first told the story of the two preachers who knew their Bibles "backwards and forwards." Their debate went:

"I cannot agree with you on Genesis xviii, 39."

"Have you considered Deuteronomy vii, 27?"

"Yes, indeed, but then how do you account for Leviticus xviii, 31?"

"By taking it in connection with Exodus vii, 42."

"You win, I hadn't thought of that."

If you are talking of a modern, neatly bound Bible, you either have to say it is a product of the Church or believe that it dropped down already-printed from heaven, as some people seem to think. All the authors of the New Testament books were certainly members of the Church. All the copyists and the people who paid them were certainly members and promoters of the Church. All the Popes and early scholarly authorities who determined what books were to be "allowed" in the Bible were certainly members of the Church. A shorter way of saying all this is to say that we got the Bible from the Church.

How the infallible Author God could use a fallible human author as His instrument is still discussed by Catholic theologians. But that God did act thus is not questioned in the Catholic Church. The Catholic position avoids rejecting any human element in Scripture, and also avoids rejecting God as Author of Scripture.

For the interpretation of the Bible text, it seems entirely reasonable to me to turn to the Church which cherished and preserved the books as they came down from the Jewish synagogues and as they were written by New Testament authors. This interpretation should be that of the magisterium of the teaching Church, not necessarily that of the latest Scripture scholars, who may very well contradict each other.

Somebody has to have the final say in matters of the Bible and the magisterium of the Church has that authority. The Pope and persons deputized by him are the equivalent of the United States Supreme Court. Neither the Church nor the country could get along without some irreversible authority. That statement is true from a purely practical viewpoint, even leaving out the consideration that the Church is under the guidance of the Holy Spirit.

Q. 34. I've always wondered why we ask God in the Lord's Prayer not to lead us into temptation, as though He sometimes did that. Can you please set me straight on this?

A. Gladly. Your theology is sounder than this part of the Lord's Prayer, though it has been recited with this phrasing by Catholics since the sixteenth century. The translation we still use was made by Henry VIII of England and imposed by him on all the churches in England. Even after Henry died and the troubles of the Reformation times abated the Catholics continued using his translation.

Henry did accurately translate the Greek and Latin forms. The mistake was made when the first written Greek Bible text did not perfectly translate the

Aramaic language our Lord spoke. Matthew wrote down what He said, but in Hebrew for which we have no text. We may never know what exact words He used, but it is generally agreed now that He would not have attributed temptation (in the strict sense of provocation to sin) to His heavenly Father.

Most translators now argue that our Lord said something like "bring us not into trial," or "do not judge us." This makes very good sense and follows naturally from the previous petition, "Forgive us our trespasses as we forgive those who trespass against us." It is as though we were saying to God "And don't be strict about how well we succeed in forgiving those who hurt us."

The Church does not change the words of the *Our Father* because most people know them by heart, and it helps public recitation to have everyone saying the same words. But, of course, the Church allows scholars to use the results of new knowledge in writing new versions of the Scriptures.

There are other inaccuracies in our form of the prayer: God is everywhere, not only "in heaven"; "daily bread" should be "bread for tomorrow" if you are to follow the Greek text, and so on. There is no end to amending the Scriptures as scholars achieve new discoveries and understandings, but it is better for most of us in daily prayer to proceed at a slower pace then the scholars.

Q. 35. What is the meaning of verse six in the seventh chapter of St. Matthew's Gospel: "Do not give dogs

what is holy; and do not throw your pearls before swine, lest they trample them underfoot and turn to attack you"?

A. I take it your problem comes from its sounding like the Lord is calling people swine and dogs, which is hard to imagine Him doing. As a matter of fact, He is warning the Apostles not to be too hasty and blunt when it comes time for them to proclaim His message. That message was so revolutionary as to sound blasphemous to devout Jews and idiotic to intellectual pagans. They were not any more likely to accept it in its fullness on first hearing than swine would appreciate a gift of pearls. Their reaction was to be so violent as to result in the death of Christ and all but one of His Apostles.

Just a few chapters further on in Matthew's Gospel, the Lord deals with the same problem in answering the Apostles when they asked why He taught in parables. He said He didn't want people to be told everything all at once—in our modern idiom, they couldn't take it. Their reaction would be only confusion and opposition.

The whole discussion is on practical means of converting people. God could certainly have made people accept everything all at once, but God's dealings are accommodated to our everyday capabilities and reactions. Our Lord used miracles, but not to overpower minds—only to persuade.

So the verse you quote does not imply that the pagans are "swine" nor that lapsed Christians are to be treated like "dogs." The true teaching was understood by the early Church. The unbaptized were excluded from the Eucharist not because they were like animals in the sight of the baptized, but because such sudden association before the pagans were properly instructed in the meaning of the ceremonies would only result in ridicule from them. Ridicule and violence were the ordinary reactions of the pagans in early Rome when they first heard of the Christian belief about eating Christ's Body and drinking his Blood.

In the verses just before the one you quote, the Lord has been telling the disciples, "Judge not, that you not be judged," and not to be hypocrites (speck of sawdust in your brother's eye, a whole log in your own). Your verse should really begin, "*But* do not give dogs what is holy; . . ." The passage leads up to the exhortation to action in verses 13 to 27. Reading it with the word *but* added in the proper place may clear up your difficulty. The teaching could be summed up, "Be zealous in preaching, but not foolishly zealous."

Q. 36. I'm confused by the passage in the Gospel of Luke which says Christ did not come into the world to bring peace but division, brother against sister, etc. Can you explain it to me?

A. Glad to try. The chapter in the Bible which included the "not peace but division" phrase (Matthew 12) is a discourse by our Lord on what is needed for salvation, what dispositions a person must have. The chapter begins with a warning by the Lord to His disciples about the danger to their faith arising from the trickery and casuistry of the Pharisees. He warns them to trust Him and not fear the judgments of His enemies.

The chapter includes the parables 1. of the lilies of the field, 2. of the silly self-satisfied rich man whose soul was required of him the night he retired to enjoy his wealth, and 3. of the faithless servant who abused his authority while his master was absent. The "not peace-but-division" phrase comes after these parables as part of the general lesson that you can't get to heaven without going counter to your usual inclinations.

The particular point of the "division-not-peace" phrase is that it told the disciples that their mission and teachings would not go unopposed. They would have to struggle and suffer in proclaiming the message of the Lord. It did not mean that the Lord had come on earth to promote war instead of peace.

Jesus was preaching in His usual style, in persuasive generalities, so that usually what He said to His relatively simple-minded hearers had to be thought upon before His meaning became crystal clear. His message was not that all would now be peace since He had come down from heaven, but that there would be a conflict between good and evil in which the disciples would be spiritual warriors.

Q. 37. Did Jesus say He was going to die for our sins? Also, if we were redeemed by Jesus' death, why is there to be a judgment?

A. Yes. In both St. Matthew's and St. Mark's Gospels He says, "The Son of Man has come, not to be served, but to serve and to give His life for the ransom of many." That's chapter 20, verse 28 in Matthew; chapter 10, verse 45 in Mark.

But the doctrine of our being redeemed by Christ's dying for our sins does not depend on the interpretation of texts of Scripture. It is the fundamental message of the Gospel and the basis of the whole Christian religion. Redemption is the master idea of the writings of St. Paul.

A quick sketch of the Catholic doctrine would begin with the observation that there is something terribly wrong with the world. Human beings do not all obey God. The resulting murders and wars must have their cause in some catastrophe at the beginning of human existence. We call it original sin. The human person is a creature endowed by the Creator with free will, the ability to turn toward the Creator with love or away from Him in disdain and disobedience. When the head of the human race did turn away from God in disobedience, it wasn't just a question of saying, "Excuse me!" to repair the damage. Infinite majesty had been offended by a finite creature, and as things stood the damage was irreparable. Nothing a human person could do would set things right. In His mercy God provided an answer. His Son became man. You have to remember that it was not just the physical death of Jesus which made up for mankind's disobedience. It was the purpose of Jesus in dying and the superhuman value of His every act as God-Man.

To answer your question about why we are to be judged even though we have been redeemed, let me point out that redemption did not take away the supreme gift of freedom of the will. A person can reject redemption even after he has accepted it at Baptism. Redemption makes salvation possible; it does not make it inevitable, nor does it guarantee it.

Q. 38. In the Bible, when reference is made to Jesus refusing to see His mother and brothers, is He being unkind to them? And who are these brothers the Bible talks about?

A. James and Joseph and Simon and Judas, according to Matthew's Gospel (13:15). But the word *brothers* is ambiguous in the languages in which the Bible was originally written. There was a single word for *relative* and *brother* so that this text does not necessarily indicate that they were blood brothers of Jesus. It could mean that they were only relatives.

Anyway, James is elsewhere called the son of Alphaeus (not the son of Joseph, spouse of the Blessed Virgin) and no one in the whole New Testament is called the son of Mary except Jesus. The Joseph in the above list is called the brother of James (not of Jesus) in both the Gospel of Matthew and that of Mark.

In a writing by Hegesippus about the year 150,

when memories of relationships would still be fresh, Simon is called the son of Clopas. Judas, the one who wrote the canonized Epistle, calls himself the brother of James (not of Jesus as one would expect if he really had that dignity). If Alphaeus and Clopas were the same person, the four could be all members of the same family. (Both *Alphaeus* and *Clopas* were variant spellings and pronunciations in Greek of the Semitic name *Halphai*.)

If you read the text of Matthew, Mark, and Luke carefully, you will see that Jesus did not seize the occasion to disgrace His brethren but only to emphasize that His work was to teach and preach to everyone without preference to those who were genetically related to Him. He was teaching that His message was for the whole world, not only for the Jews as some of His followers mistakenly thought. An added thought is that our Lord was not always "all smiles." His denunciations of the money changers, the Pharisees, and of Judas Iscariot the traitor indicate that His attitudes and expressions were those of the true human nature which was His.

Q. 39. Why is "For Thine is the kingdom and the power and the glory forever" not included in the Lord's prayer as it is taught in Catholic books and pamphlets?

A. It's a matter of what is called textual criticism. Scholars try but they can never get exactly to what any author of Scripture originally wrote because none of the pieces of sheepskin or whatever they wrote on exist anymore. All the scholars have to work on is copies made centuries ago. For instance, St. Paul just dictated some of his letters, which was a common practice in ancient times, so the best version we can possibly have is what his secretary thought Paul had said. Paul signed his letters but we have no certainty that he proofread them and eliminated all errors. When his letter was copied for us in churches other than the one to which he sent the letter, the chance of further errors creeping in to the text increased. Down the centuries, in this process of copying by hand, some errors would be corrected, others would be repeated. What are called families of manuscripts developed.

In the case of the passage in the sixth chapter of Matthew (where our Lord taught the Apostles the Lord's Prayer) some manuscripts included *For Thine* . . . and others did not, according to which family they belonged. With the invention of printing, Protestant Bibles followed the family that included the words "For Thine . . .," while Catholic Bible editors, upon the advice of the Catholic scholars, excluded them as being a pious comment written into the text by an early copier. Modern versions of the Bibles approved for both Protestants and Catholics leave the words out; only reprints of the King James Bible have them now. But they were beautiful words, a quotation from the First Book of Chronicles. And the Church put them into the Missal of 1963, not as an integral part of the Lord's Prayer, which was already perfect, but as a response by the people to the priest's prayer following the Lord's Prayer.

Q. 40. Can you explain why Jesus on the cross said, "My God, My God, why have You forsaken Me?"

A. It does sound like a cry of despair and makes one wonder at first why the evangelists who wrote it down did so if they were trying to make people believe Christ was divine. But the followers of Christ who heard and reported His words knew that He was quoting a psalm and not "making up" the words Himself. Christ was praying and these words are only the first verse of a long psalm that He was reciting. It is Psalm 22 (21 in older Bibles).

The psalmist is writing poetry and in the first verse expresses his feeling that God had deserted him. Later on in the psalm it becomes clear that God did not turn His face away and that the poem as a whole is an expression of supreme confidence in God's mercy. It was therefore not a complaint or cry of despair.

The opening words, "My God, my God," are *Eloi, Eloi,* in the Aramaic language our Lord spoke. The enemies of Christ made a joke out of them because they sounded something like Elijah, the name of the great prophet whose return the Jews expected. "Behold, He is calling Elijah," they said. Even the bystander who offered Jesus the sour wine (vinegar) went along with the joke, saying, "Wait, let us see if Elijah will come to take Him down."

Of course, the Lord Himself was the "Elijah" or

Messiah that Israel was awaiting, but the nation did not recognize Him in the "Criminal" it saw dying on the cross. The Lord spoke Psalm 22 to show that the prayer and suffering of the psalmist were fore-shadowings of His own messiahship. It could also have been that our Lord chose to recite this psalm (a psalm asking an unanswerable why) in His dying minutes, to show that suffering is not necessarily a punishment for individual sin but part of some mysterious providence of God, since the sinless Christ endured it.

But the most likely reason for His choosing this psalm to recite would be its text, "They tear holes in My hands and My feet and lay Me in the dust of death. I can count every one of My bones. These people stare at Me and gloat; they divide My clothing among them, they cast lots for My robe." Like the passage in Isaiah (chapter 52, verse 13, to chapter 53, verse 12) this passage almost seems to be that of an eyewitness of the crucifixion scene. But it was written by one who lived centuries before the events he describes. Christ's death fulfilled the Scripture and He was quoting that Scripture as He died.

Q. 41. The Bible vividly describes the part the Jews played in the crucifixion of Christ. As the texts read, it sounds as though the whole race and religion of the Jews approved of it, but surely there were some who did not. Shouldn't the Church publicize the fact that not all the Jews hated Christ?

A. You're right. But before holding anything against the Church consider that the Church itself never held the Jews as a race accountable any more than our Lord did. The New Testament tells us that three thousand Jews were converted on Pentecost, which on top of the circumstance that Christ and His Apostles were all Jews makes it nonsense to hold the race guilty.

But it is true that much of the anti-Semitism the world has witnessed, that of the Nazis as well as the medieval Christians, derives specifically from St. John's Gospel where the unqualified "Jews" are presented as enemies of Christ. But St. John did not intend to stir up race hatred. It was private inter-preters of the Bible, looking for texts that would reinforce their prejudices, and careless preachers who caused unthinking Christians to hate "the Jews."

St. John wrote his Gospel decades after the death of Christ at a time when the Jews dispersed through the world were becoming either fervent Christians or active anti-Christians intent on preserving the old religion of Moses. It was natural for him to call his opponents "the Jews," even though he could just as reasonably refer to himself and most of his fellow Christians as Jews.

By the time John wrote there was no longer any question of compromise, such as was considered by the Council of Jerusalem, between the New and the Old Law. It had to be one or the other. "The Jews" was the most intelligible and aptest name with which to label the followers of the Old Law. That private interpreters of the Bible misused John's term for his theological opponents as an excuse for their own hatred of a whole race has become regrettable to the point of horror.

Q. 42. Is Luke's Gospel really an eyewitness account?

A. Luke was a great literary artist in the construction of his Gospel message, beginning and ending it in the Temple of Jerusalem, for instance. He was a master of language, writing in much better Greek than comes to us in the translations of the Hebrew and Aramaic Gospels, and he had no difficulty with the idioms of his Hebrew and Aramaic sources. These skills could make it seem to the reader that Luke was a witness of all he told.

He says at the very beginning of his Gospel that there were many (i.e. not just Matthew and Mark) who had written about what they as eyewitnesses saw of the life of Christ. The clear implication is that he sifted out and himself used the materials and details which in his judgment should be preserved in his "orderly account." He intended to strengthen the faith of persons already converted, rather than to bring the first news to anyone about Christ. Accordingly, his narrative is reassuring and persuasive.

And the best way to be reassuring and persuasive is to give the effect of an eyewitness account. To this end he obviously interviewed eyewitnesses. By twice telling us in the same chapter (two) that "Mary pondered these things in her heart," he strongly implies that the Blessed Mother was one of his interviewees, and there is no reason to doubt that she was. Luke could thus learn the exact words that Mary exchanged with the angel at the Annunciation.

Q. 43. In Colossians 1:24, St. Paul says, "In my own flesh I will make up what is lacking in the sufferings of Christ for the sake of His body, the Church." What could possibly be lacking in Christ's suffering?

A. In the Revised Standard Version (Catholic edition) there is a note on that word *lacking.* The notes in the New American Bible which you are using do not cover it. The RSV note reads, "Christ's sufferings were, of course, sufficient for our redemption, but all of us may add ours to His, in order that the fruits of His redemption be applied to the souls of men."

Our sufferings (of only finite value) can be added in God's arithmetic to the infinitely valuable sufferings of Jesus because we are one with Him in His Mystical Body, the Church. He the head suffered, we the members can suffer. To our human minds the total suffering would seem to be more than that of Christ alone, so that the use of the word *lacking* would be permissible as long as we do not call the merits of Christ's suffering less than infinite.

But our suffering, unlike that of Christ, is not of itself meritorius. It did the bad thief no good at the crucifixion. The suffering of the damned does not expiate sin. It is only when our suffering is willingly accepted in obedience to God's will that it can make up "what is lacking" in the sufferings of Christ. It has then become precious and of the same nature as Christ's suffering. Why Christ chose suffering as the instrument of our salvation must remain a mystery to us, but we know that while comfortable obedience to God is a good thing, obedience while suffering is heroic. St. Paul found his joy in it.

Q. 44. Who is the Antichrist?

A. Astrologers claim that the Antichrist will come during a conjunction of Jupiter with the moon, but they do not say who he will be.

Apocryphal literature, the pseudo-Scripture, says he is Belial. This is Satan himself, according to the Vulgate translation of the Bible. In the Old Testament Belial is a kind of personification of all evil, but the term *Antichrist* does not appear. If you want to stay in the New Testament, specifically in Revelation, to find the Antichrist you have a wide choice of monsters besides the beast mentioned in the Book of Revelation.

But, before you make any choice, you ought to look into the term *Antichrist* to see how the Catholic Church arrived at its teaching that he will be a human enemy of Christ who will come only in the last days of the world.

First of all, he is named only in the Epistles of St. John. No other writer of Scripture uses the term *Antichrist,* but Catholic teaching identifies him with "the man of sin" St. Paul talks about in his Second Letter to the Thessalonians. In fact, there is strong opinion that John first heard of such an archenemy from the preaching or writing of St. Paul. St. Paul, in turn, surely knew about the enemy of God portrayed by Ezekiel (chapters 38, 39) and by Daniel (chapters 7, 8). Of course, the mistaken idea that there are two equal gods, one good and one bad, is the basis of several ancient religions, and St. Paul may even have been accommodating a pagan false teaching to Christian truth.

In any event, the term *Antichrist* comes to us from St. John and you ought to get its meaning from him.

In his First Letter, St. John says that not only those who will read his letter will have already heard that the Antichrist is coming, but also that many Antichrists have already come. These Antichrists are evidently some people who joined the Church but then left it and did so denying Christ. But he speaks also of *the* Antichrist in the singular and as though the last hours of the world were at hand as he (John) was writing. This is where we get the idea that the Antichrist will come only as the world approaches its end.

In his Second Letter, John speaks of the Antichrist as one who will "not acknowledge the coming of the Lord Jesus Christ in the flesh." That is where we get the Catholic teaching that the Antichrist must be the one whom St. Paul calls "the man of sin, who opposes . . . all that is called God." This man of sin, St. Paul says, will be destroyed by Christ at His (second) coming, at the end of the world. Apart from this we don't know much about the Antichrist.

But the Church is against the idea that *the* Antichrist is a character in past human history or even one of our own time, unless the world is indeed nearing its grand finale.

Q. 45. Noah's Ark has always been a puzzle to me. I can't understand how all the animals could have gotten on the Ark. What do you think?

A. As a matter of fact, it very probably did not happen if you are taking the Genesis text to mean that hundreds of thousands of animals boarded the Ark. Persons who take the words that literally don't know or notice that the word *all* is used throughout the story (and in ancient writings generally) for only portions of what the *all* would be. For example, Noah is called a just man (one made of flesh) but the text says that *all* flesh had "corrupted its way." It says that *all* men perished in the waters, while the point of the whole story is that the man Noah and his family did not perish.

We use the same idiom in everyday speech when we say something like "Those mosquitos are everywhere." We don't really mean they are on the moon or the far reaches of the universe, we just mean that there are a lot of them in our yard. We use a "universal" expression to make our statement stronger.

The writer of the text in Genesis who was quoting God meant that Noah was to put on the ark all the domestic animals it could accommodate. It is impossible that the writer of the text could have known about the millions of species of wild animals and believed that God put the obligation on Noah of taking some of each along with them.

Difficulties like the one you cited stem from certain denominations arising after the establishment of the Bible as the sole rule of Protestant faith. They extended the true idea that the Bible was right to the false idea that every word, even in translations, was to be taken literally.

Q. 46. Who was Melchizedek? Some friends of mine believe that he was the second member of the Godhead who later gave up divinity to become Jesus Christ of Nazareth.

A. We believe Melchizedek was king of Salem, just like it says in the Book of Genesis. In the ancient times of Abraham being the king meant being the priest of the tribe as well. Melchizedek was not a Hebrew but a Jebusite, a member of the tribe that owned the land long before the Hebrews took over and renamed it Salem. It became Jerusalem.

In the Bible story, Lot, a kinsman of Abraham, had been captured in one of the wars between groups of petty kings. Abraham defeated Lot's captors, and, with only three hundred eighteen men, took all the booty of his enemies and restored it to its owners. The priest-king Melchizedek "brought out bread and wine" and blessed Abraham. The Roman Canon of the Mass refers to his action as a sacrifice. The Jebusites' name for God, *El*, was the same as the Hebrew name for God, so the supposition is that

Melchizedek worshiped the true God, not one of the heathen deities.

What probably led your friends astray was the identification of the priesthood of Christ with the priesthood of Melchizedek by the author of the Epistle to the Hebrews. Your friends seem to have Godhood mixed up with priesthood. All the Epistle says is that Christ was a priest "according to the order of Melchizedek." It does not say He was the same person as Melchizedek.

Scholars tell us that the story of Melchizedek looks like it was inserted into an earlier text of Genesis. The purpose of the inserters would have been to bolster the authority of the Jewish kings who succeeded Melchizedek in Jerusalem. They wanted to be priest-kings with a line of succession going back beyond David (who took the city) to the very time of Abraham, father of the Jewish race. Such an insertion would account for Melchizedek not being mentioned anywhere in Genesis except in this one place. The author of the Epistle to the Hebrews, instead of seeing Melchizedek as the first of the Jewish priests, concluded from Melchizedek's uniqueness that his priesthood was of a higher order.

Q. 47. What am I to make of certain Christians who ask me to furnish Biblical proofs of Catholic doctrines such as the infallibility of the Pope and purgatory? My Catholic background is a little shaky at this point.

A. Brace up. The Catholic Church has such love and reverence for the Holy Scriptures that many Catholics including yourself accept without question the idea that the Bible is the *only* source of true Christian religion. Like you, without knowing the proofs of their own beliefs, they presume that someone or other of the Doctors or Fathers of the Church have furnished proofs from the Bible for every Catholic tenet and position.

This is not the case and need not be the case. The totality of Catholic faith is based on the Scriptures, the use of human reason, historical traditions, and the inspiration of the Holy Spirit.

With persons who insist that the Bible should be the *only* source of Christian doctrine you begin by asking where they got that tenet. There are plenty of texts in the Bible which say the Scriptures should be reverenced and studied (as the Catholic Church holds) but no text saying that *only* the Bible can be used as a test of religious truth. How could there be such a test? The Bible text nowhere has a table of its own contents so that a reader could tell what is truly "Bible" and what is not.

Beginning with the fact that the Lord Himself didn't *write* any of the Bible, going on to the fact that the Bible books were not collected into a single volume for several centuries after Christ, and to the fact that even casual perusal of the Bible was not possible for more than 99 percent of the Christian population until the invention of printing in the fifteenth century, it would seem unlikely that God should judge people on their Christian beliefs on the basis of the Bible *alone.*

Q. 48. The story of Jacob's deception in Genesis 27 has always bothered me. Why was this story included in the Bible if to "tell a lie" is truly a sin?

A. For those without a Bible at hand, let me say first that *Genesis 25* has the story of Jacob buying his twin but elder brother's birthright and then deceiving his aged and blind father into giving him the privileges, priorities, and social advantages that the first-born son had in those patriarchal times.

As the story is told there is no doubt that Jacob lied; the difficulty is that the narrator seems to approve. But when you look to the complete teaching as it is unfolded in Jacob's life story you will find that Jacob was punished in his lifetime for the deception and that the narrator is not approving lying but showing that it is wrong. He tells how Jacob was in turn deceived by his uncle, Laban, into working for seven years in exchange for having Rachel as his wife, only to find the morning after the wedding that the veiled bride was not Rachel whom he loved but Leah, her older sister. He had to work another seven years to get Rachel.

Some Church Fathers, medieval rabbis, and even St. Augustine did not see it this way but found excuses for Jacob's lie. St. Augustine says it was not a lie but a mystery, a story intended by the narrator to foreshadow the supplanting of the Jewish religion by Christ, as Jacob supplanted Esau. Other commentators have said that the story is so old that it goes back to the times when there was not much connection between morals and religious observances (as with some present-day religious fanatics).

Others say that Isaac, the father of the twins, knew all along that it was Jacob disguised as Esau but went through with the transfer of the birthright because of some special revelation from God that Jacob should be preferred for his qualities of leadership. Some even think that the whole story was intended as a farce in which lying would not matter. The humorous elements would include the cleverness of Jacob, the buffoonery of the uncouth Esau, the bumbling of the older gaffer Isaac, and the machination of Rebecca. But none of these considerations excuse the real lie.

Q. 49. Did anyone ever see God face to face? What about Moses in Exodus 34, who took off his veil when he was speaking to God?

A. Yes and no. God does not have a face, except in the Incarnation of Jesus Christ. And the revelation of the Trinity had not yet been made in Moses' time. In Exodus, chapter 33, verse 20, God says to Moses, "You cannot see My face for man shall not see Me and live." But our metaphorical expression "face to face" means the closest kind of communication possible, and Moses did have that. The expression is used in Catholic devotion in the belief that we shall see God "face to face" at Judgment and in heaven. But Moses, even in receiving the Ten Commandments, did not have that close an encounter with God.

Characters in the Old Testament often mention the common belief of the people then that one could not see God and live. God used the sensory faculties of His prophets to communicate with them, so that they reported hearing God speak or seeing some kind of presence—such as the burning bush Moses saw or the cloud on Mount Sinai at Moses' reception of the Ten Commandments. But the prophets did not use the expression "face to face" or any other anthropomorphic term in describing their encounters with the Almighty.

In New Testament times, Paul was blinded by the light from heaven before Christ asked him, "Why persecutest thou Me?" Paul gave no description in visual terms of what his encounter was like. Other saints have had visions of Christ but have not described Him as they would be able to describe another human being whom they have met "face to face." The great mystics of the Church who have reached the unitive way ("contemplating the face of God," so to speak) invariably have said that their visions of the Trinity are indescribable.

And, of course, John in his Gospel, chapter 1, verse 18, says, "No one has ever seen God . . ."

Q. 50. I'd like to learn more about the Ark of the Covenant. Can you tell me about it?

A. God told Moses that He wanted him to construct a tabernacle and an ark for the religious use of the people. God's command was carried out within a year of the deliverance of the Hebrews from Egypt. The Ark lasted nearly nine hundred years, from the deliverance from Egypt in about 1400 B.C. to the destruction of Solomon's temple in 537 B.C.

You can read about God's instructions in the twenty-fifth chapter of the Book of Exodus. The artisan Beseleel made the Ark, a box five to six feet long and about three feet wide and high. It was fitted with four rings through which two poles could be inserted for carrying. The whole Ark, the rings, and the poles were overlaid with pure gold. Two golden angels (cherubim) faced each other from the ends of the Ark with their wings spread over the central part of the cover called the Mercy Seat. In it were placed the stone tablets of the Law, the rod of Aaron, and a golden vessel holding some of the manna that fell in the desert.

The Mercy Seat was the focal point of Jewish worship, the place which God made His specific dwelling place with His people.

The Ark was carried each day in the van of the people during their forty years wandering in the desert. When the conquest of the promised land was accomplished, the Ark was kept at Shiloh in the geographical center of the country. It was moved about for special occasions and in military campaigns. Once it was captured and returned.

When Solomon constructed his temple, it was kept there and vanished from history when that temple was destroyed by the Babylonians. There is a Jewish tradition that the prophet Jeremiah was forewarned of the destruction of the temple and that he took the Ark to Mount Sinai, where Moses received the Ten Commandments, placed it in a cave there and filled the entrance so no one could find it. Another tradition was that it was included in the booty of the Babylonians; still another that it was safely hidden by King Josiah deep in the foundations of the Temple and that it would be found at the coming of the Messiah.

Old Testament miracles occurred in connection with the Ark. The river Jordan dried up at its approach at the siege of Jericho. When it was captured it was placed in the temple of the pagan god Dagon, whose statue fell and broke to pieces in its presence. A plague and then an explosion of the mouse population broke out in the territory of those who had captured it, so they sent it back to the Hebrews. Its power was shown once after it was returned when in the course of the victory procession, the oxen pulling its cart slipped and a man was struck dead just for reaching out and touching the Ark to make sure it would not fall to the ground. But after it was in Jewish possession for a while, it brought only blessings. And King David kept it in Jerusalem where it remained until the building and later destruction of the first Temple.

CHAPTER FIVE

DEATH, PURGATORY, AND THE LAST THINGS

*Questions on praying for death,
cremation, purgatory,
the reuniting of the body and soul at
the Last Judgment,
and who are the dead Christ is going to judge
when He comes again.*

Death, Purgatory, and the Last Things

Q. 51. I have been told by a priest that it is wrong to pray for death, either for oneself or another. Can we ever pray for death?

A. Before I say Yes, let me explain that if you *pray* in the strict sense of that word, you can pray for anything. "To pray" is to lift your heart and mind to God.

For example, parts of what are known as the "vindictive" psalms of the Bible have been omitted from the new breviary because the prayer was for such things as that the children of the Babylonians be dashed against the rock. Christian prayer for such things doesn't make sense. But the pre-Christian author of that vindictive psalm thought he was honoring God in uttering such a prayer, since the prayer was to the true God, spoken for the benefit of

God's chosen people, and did not really have injury to helpless infants as its main motive.

Praying for death is like that. It is not really death that is desired but only the relief from pain or care that it brings, relief which is thought of as being obtainable in no other way. So we can pray for death as long as the main motive is not the specific rejection of God's gift of life.

Persistence in prayer will usually boil one's thought down to one's utter dependence on the Creator. At that point requests for special benefits, or for preference over others, or for things ordinarily injurious to self or others lose relevance because they are part of *our* will. All that matters is God's will. The essence of our prayer must be that our free will be conformed to God's, which gets us back to the point that if prayer is sincere we can ask for anything we feel like. We won't ask for anything that will not be to the glory of God. "Love God and do what you will" is another way of saying it.

Q. 52. Is it still true that Catholics are not supposed to be cremated?

A. Yes, the *attitude* of the church toward cremation has not changed. But many *rules* were changed in 1963. Penalties for those who arranged cremations were removed if permission was first received from the bishop and there was no intention of denying the Resurrection of the Body by the act of cremation.

The Church has always recognized that there are

circumstances which should allow cremation. Exceptions to the old rules are routinely made in case of plague and war for reasons of hygiene.

In many places this reason could still be applicable. It is understandable that for some families the difference in expense now between cremation and formal burial could be a sufficient reason. Even the high cost of cemetery lots could be a factor in great cities. Hygiene and cost do not exhaust the list of reasonable excuses. But the Church does not encourage cremation. Many dioceses require that a letter be sent to the bishop by the person (before his death, of course) who wants to be cremated giving his reason, stating that he has no intention of denying the Resurrection, and directing that his ashes be sealed in a container and buried or left in a mausoleum.

It is also generally required that the body of the deceased be brought to the church for the Mass of Christian Burial. If this cannot be done, a memorial Mass may be offered but the ashes may not be substituted for the body in the regular funeral ceremonies. A specific ceremony at the crematorium is provided for in the instruction issued in 1967.

The Church's opposition to cremation began with the burning of early Christian martyrs. Roman emperors scattered their ashes to ridicule Christian belief in the Resurrection. There was an echo of this type of ridicule in anticlerical societies of the last century which were formed to encourage cremation as a sign of contempt for all religious belief.

Romantic requests for the scattering of ashes over

favorite beauty spots are expressions of pagan pan-
theism which have led to the present general Catholic
insistence on the disposition of ashes in a cemetery lot
or a mausoleum. Civil law in some states, including
California, forbids the scattering of human ashes.
There was a touch of macabre humor in the effort of a
Reno cemetery manager to have such a law passed in
Nevada, because a crematorium in California was
advertising an airplane service using Nevada's moun-
tains as disposal areas.

But the Church's preference for burial and opposition to cremation are not entirely accounted for by
what Roman persecutors, religious skeptics, or pan-
theists did. As in the case of other Catholic practices
such as celibacy of the clergy and the use of bread and
wine for the Eucharist, the example of Christ Himself
is at the bottom of it all. Christ "died and was buried."

When He rose from the dead, He was recognizably
Himself, doing things like eating food with the
Apostles and making Thomas feel the wounds in His
hands and side. Had His body been cremated or
otherwise destroyed He still could have done all this
by the exercise of His almighty power, but to teach the
doctrine of the Resurrection to the ordinary people of
His own time, He appeared to them in the familiar
form that they had known. He made the miracle
simple—He died and rose to life—He was not
teaching abstractions that only philosophers could
easily follow.

This example of the Lord is the source of the
Church's reverence for the deceased human body.

The Church holds to this reverence in the face of the fact that no one can be sure of rising in an undestroyed body. The earth and all the human remains in it will ultimately be vaporized by an aging and expanding sun. Atomic physicists tell us that even inanimate matter is interchangeable with pure energy, so that the atoms and molecules that make up our human bodies may even be said to go in and out of the real of matter as we know it.

We don't know just how God will proceed in restoring our remains so that we, too, will be recognizably ourselves, but we are by faith sure that He can and will do so. St. Thomas, though speaking on his own human authority and not from special revelation from God, assures us that everyone who gets to heaven will have a perfect body at the best possible age of life which he specifies as thirty-three, our Lord's age at His death.

The Church's insistence on traditional burial is based on devotion to the example of Christ. His disciples saw and recognized Him in His body, changed from what they had seen before His death, but changed in the direction of glory, not toward dissolution or decay.

Q. 53. Is there such a place as purgatory?

A. You have to accept purgatory if you believe that God is perfectly just. His justice is not always apparent here on earth: often the wicked prosper and die happy, sometimes with sorrow for their sins but without ever having suffered any punishment at all. Would a perfectly just God take them directly to heaven just as He would someone who gave up a saintly life in defense of God's name? The Church doesn't say that the once-wicked person never gets to heaven (having repented his sins), but does say he goes to purgatory for enough punishment to satisfy the infinite justice for God.

When Christians—who believe they are sure of heaven as soon as they are "saved" here on earth—say that God is also perfectly merciful and *would* take the repentant sinner straight to heaven, your answer is that God's justice is satisfied *if* that happens by the merits of Christ and the good things the saints did in addition to those which won them salvation. God applies these merits to the sinner and perfect justice is wrought.

This line of thought brings in another Catholic doctrine which is proclaimed every time the Creed is recited at Mass: the Communion of Saints. Purgatory is an integral part of this doctrine, which affirms that the force of Christian love can be exerted beyond the grave, that the saints in heaven can help persons still on earth or in purgatory by their intercessions before God, and that we can help those in purgatory and honor the saints in heaven by our prayers.

Any discussion of purgatory must include the Catholic teaching that the Mass is a sacrifice, that it is more than a get-together, more than an occasion for Bible reading, more than an occasion to remember the life of Christ. It is indeed a re-enactment of what occurred on the cross, and the Lord must have had some reason for making it that.

Catholics find the reason partly, at least, in purgatory. As a repeatable re-enactment, the once-and-for-all sacrifice of Christ can be applied for individual benefits in individual Masses. We can deal with infinite values in terms which our finite human minds can more easily grasp. If you don't mind a crude analogy, had Christ not made his sacrifice re-enactable it would have been like a billion-dollar insurance policy, payable only at our death. The way He arranged things we are more in the position of having inexhaustible checking accounts upon which we can draw here and now to help the souls in purgatory.

Christ was thinking of the souls in purgatory at the Last Supper when He planned His sacrifice so that we could have our part in it through the Mass. There are so many doctrines on the Church which presuppose the existence of a nonpermanent state after death—at least for some souls—that you cannot be a Catholic without believing in purgatory. If you had been brought up as your Protestant friends were, to believe that none of the doctrines we mentioned above are true, it would take some kind of miracle to get you to believe in purgatory.

But within the Church, believers should have some kind of separate basis for this doctrine. It was formulated at the Council of Trent: "The Catholic Church, instructed by the Holy Spirit, by the Sacred Scriptures and the ancient tradition of the Fathers, has taught in Sacred Councils, and very recently in this

Ecumenical Synod, that there is a purgatory, and that the souls therein detained are helped by all the prayer of the faithful, but principally by the acceptable sacrifice of the altar.''

Maybe you noticed immediately, that the document plainly says that the Council uses the Scriptures as a source of its teaching on purgatory. Of course, the word *purgatory* as a proper noun is not in the Scriptures. As a common noun it once meant a place of cleaning or expiating. I dare to suppose that it never was used as a proper noun for a state of suffering until, in the controversies with Protestants over the doctrine, it became a handy shortcut in speaking of whole concepts.

This concept of an intermediate state between earth and heaven *is* in the Catholic Scriptures, the Second Book of Maccabees, which Protestants do not acknowledge as part of the Bible. The Anglicans have Bibles which include this book with the note that it must not be used for the basis of doctrine.

The passage which makes the Second Book of Maccabees unacceptable to the opponents of purgatory reads, "Therefore he made atonement for the dead that they might be delivered from their sin" (in chapter 12, verse 45). What had happened was that the Jewish general Judas Maccabeus had lost some men in a battle with the Idumeans. When the time came to bury them with proper honors, they were found to be carrying tokens of idols, a sin in the Jewish religion. Judas took up a collection from his soldiers which amounted to 2,000 drachmas and sent it to the priests in Jerusalem to provide sacrifices to expiate their sin. The Catholic practice of having Masses offered for the souls in purgatory is pretty much the same thing as what Judas did, and what he did *is* in the Catholic Scriptures. Clearly, pious Jews of Biblical times prayed for their dead.

In the Gospel of Matthew, which is in both the Catholic and Protestant Scriptures, our Lord says, "Whoever speaks against the Holy Spirit will not be forgiven, either in this world or in the world to come." This text indirectly indicates that there is a purgatory.

Some of the new translations use *age* instead of *world* but doing so blurs the force of this text a little. The King James and Authorized versions (Protestant), as well as the Catholic Rheims-Douay version, had *world;* the Revised Standard version changed *world* to *age.* I prefer *world* because our argument is that if there is a sin which will not be forgiven in this world *or* in the next world, there must be some sins which are forgiven in the next world.

That would have to be done in a purgatory, not in heaven or hell. It isn't really an argument which bowls anyone over, but it was used by the Fathers of the Church in defense of the doctrine of purgatory, notably by St. Augustine, Gregory the Great, St. Bede, St. Bernard, and Isadore of Seville.

It leaves to be proven that remission of the punishment does not come with the forgiving of the sin. Some Protestants teach that it does come then. But that is where the Catholic teaching that God is perfectly just *and* perfectly merciful comes in: mercy and the grace of contrition are always extended while the person is alive; at his death perfect justice is wrought. The teaching of "no purgatory" overlooks or disregards the perfect justice of God.

There is one more argument drawn from Scripture, 1 Corinthians, chapter 3, verses 11 to 15. The text is to the effect that in the judgment every person's work will be tested by fire, but it says that even though the work is burned, the sinner will survive. There is much, much more to the text than that and it is difficult to interpret and translate clearly from the Greek. But the Fathers used the argument on the basis of the text reading they had. Because of the obscurity of the text, we had better not place too much trust in its ability to convert anyone to the doctrine of purgatory.

The Catholic Church says the Bible itself is only a part of Tradition, since the traditions guided Church members before the New Testament was even written and for about 1,600 years before the complete Bible was physically available to the average follower of Christ seeking further knowledge of Christian doctrine. The writers of Scripture, inspired by God, wrote down what they did to preserve traditions. They were not attempting to write down an exhaustive treatment of the teaching of Christ. They were not compiling a textbook.

So we get the doctrine of purgatory from tradition as well as from Scripture. The Fathers of the Church, as we saw, routinely taught the doctrine and didn't even have much opposition until the Reformation. In pre-Protestant times the Greek Orthodox Church, which now rejects purgatory, differed from the Catholic Church only on the nature of purgatorial fire. There were also a few heretics like the Albigensians, Waldensians, and Jussites, who seemed to oppose everything Catholic as a matter of principle, but their influence was only local.

There is a kind of reasonableness about inevitable punishment for crime that has supported the doctrine of purgatory among Catholics. Certainly there is no sin or trace of sin in heaven where the saints are in the presence of the Beatific Vision of God. Yet we know that many persons die in venial sin which will not send them, surely, to hell forever. There has to be a purgatory for them and for the imperfectly penitent mortal sinners who have not suffered in any way at all for their misdeeds.

The Catholic Church has always taught that immediate heaven is possible for some persons: perfect contrition remits all sin *and* all punishment. One who is sorry for his sin only because of its offense to the infinitely good God and not at all because he must suffer punishment for it can be assured of immediate heaven. Catholic theologians differ among themselves on whether perfect contrition is an easy or very difficult accomplishment. In any case, purgatory is part of God's mercy for those who cannot achieve perfect sorrow.

The idea of a place of non-eternal punishment is not exclusively Catholic. As we saw, Judas Maccabeus and the Pharisees had the thought. The Hindus believe in reincarnations. These are repeated purgatories on the way to final extinction. Mormons say they do not believe in purgatory, but they believe in baptisms for the dead—a change certainly in spiritual status after death. Scholars have found hints of this purgatorial belief even in the writings of Virgil and Sophocles.

Q. 54. How will body and soul be reunited at the Last Judgment? What about those whose bodies have been cremated?

A. I don't think anyone knows, nor has the Church defined, *how* body and soul will be reunited, except to say it will be through the power of God. Your statement of the difficulty can be enlarged upon. Through natural decay or destruction by fire the components of the deceased human body are certainly beyond any human reconstruction. But even during life on earth, the human body does not have the same material particles in it from minute to minute, let alone from year to year. The particles to which its elements can be reduced are not "solid." According to subatomic science, they are forms of charges of electricity, interchanging, coming and going. The human body by the replacement and rearrangement of these particles, hears, sees, and reacts.

We have to ask, in speaking of the reunion of the immortal soul with this arrangement of subatomic particles we call the body, which of the billions of arrangements of particles it had on earth will be resurrected.

We know that Christ's resurrected body was identifiable, but it was not immediately recognizable. Our resurrected bodies will be like Christ's. They will have an identity with those we had in earthly life, without necessarily having the identical physical components which would be "scientifically" impossible. Our bodies will be glorified as with Christ's, each will be perfect, mature, and unimpaired by length of years.

All of this will be accomplished, not by any retrieval of atoms and reconstruction of electrical particles, which is the only way our finite human minds can think of resurrection, but by a new creation. As the Bible says, "Behold, I make all things new" (Book of Revelation, chapter 21, verse 5).

Q. 55. Who are the dead Christ is going to judge when He comes again? Haven't people who have died already been judged?

A. Everybody who ever lived. The good old Baltimore Catechism says that there are two judgments, the particular and the general. The first occurs at the death of the person and the second at the end of the present world.

The Baltimore Catechism, based on the Catechism of the Council of Trent, explains that the general judgment, which is for all on the same day and place, is part of the punishment of the wicked and part of the reward of the good. Each person's judgment then will be in the hearing and presence of everyone who ever lived. So the "dead" at the Last Judgment will be literally everybody.

It is much harder to answer the question of who the "living" will be, in view of the scientific certainty that our planet will be destroyed when our sun suffers the fate of every other star. The text of the Profession of Faith dates from times when nothing was known about these scientific aspects, and its authors simply assumed some action on the part of God which ended the world without killing everybody. Apparently they did not, at the time of composing the Profession, have in mind the necessity for death brought on by original sin. The overriding consideration is that the general judgment will take place in "eternity," not in "time" which is part of the present creation, so that to our limited human understanding, the two judgments could be simultaneous. Both *living* and *dead* could be properly applied to each person at the general judgment because it will take place in eternity, where there is no succession of events, one after the other, as there is in time. But the simplest and sanest explanation is that "the living and the dead" is just a fancy or literary way of saying "everybody."

CHAPTER SIX

SIN AND SATAN

*Questions on the differences between mortal
and venial sin,
the unpardonable sin,
the existence of Satan and evil spirits,
and the Black Mass.*

Sin and Satan

Q. 56. Our son has just received the sacraments of Penance and First Communion, yet he hasn't received any instruction about mortal and venial sin. When will he become capable of mortal sin and how do we describe the difference between mortal and venial to him?

A. The old Baltimore Catechism came about as close as anyone could to defining mortal sin: there has to be 1. grievous matter, 2. sufficient reflection, and 3. full consent of the will.

The trouble with that explanation is that it only removes the difficulties by one stage. You have then to determine what is meant by *grievous, sufficient,* and *full.* It's about the same problem as extracting the square root of two, no matter how far you investigate there are always further considerations to be made so that in the case of another person's sin, no one can ever be certain whether it was mortal or venial. Certainly, mortal sin *is* possible but only the person committing it can be the final judge of whether it was mortal or venial.

Now, to get this across to a child, in fact to a person of any age, is difficult, so catechists of vintage more recent than the Baltimore Catechism have taken the position that it is better simply to oppose *all* sin, in instructing children. If done competently, this will keep them from mortal sin.

The old rule-of-thumb laws, such as the one which specified a day's wages as the criterion for mortal in matters of theft, really didn't hold for all cases. But by not mentioning mortal sin, the more modern approach has the real danger of minimizing the sense of sin.

Modern "thinkers" check off the sense of sin as a psychoneurosis, but the lack of guilt feelings is obviously what is the matter with the modern world and what has been the matter with the world since the creation of Adam and Eve. Instilling in the child a horror of mortal sin, along with the implication that it was quite possible to commit it (as the old Baltimore Catechism did), may be instilling a neurosis, but it does give him the information that it is in his power to separate himself from God—forever. The dread possibility may never occur to a child left to his own judgments.

Q. 57. I know that procuring abortion carries the penalty of automatic excommunication. Is this the unpardonable sin for which there is no forgiveness?

A. It does not mean that. The sin that will not be forgiven was spoken of by our Lord in the Gospel of Matthew, chapter 12, verses 31 and 32. It is blasphemy against the Holy Spirit which is generally interpreted to mean that the person committing it has refused the grace of God through the moment of death, so that he is finally impenitent. The sin is unforgivable because the sinner refuses forgiveness.

The automatic excommunication of Canon 1398 can be removed by the bishop or through a priest who has been given faculties to absolve the sin, or in urgent cases even by the first priest to hear a sincere confession of the sin, if the penitent promises to come back to get the formal absolution of the bishop which the priest will ask for in the meantime. In this case the sinner is not refusing forgiveness but asking for it.

The Church makes the penalty for abortion automatic excommunication because the harm done cannot be humanly repaired. For that reason, in the case of deliberate abortion, the sin has a malice above and beyond that of most human failings. The child is denied Baptism, which in God's Providence is the ordinary way of getting to heaven. For anyone with normal human sensibilities and this Christian belief, the remorse is very nearly unbearable. But the sin can be forgiven because God's mercy is infinite.

Q. 58. What does the Catholic Church say about the existence of Satan or the devil and evil spirits?

A. To begin with, a Catholic does not have to believe in the popular notion of the devil—a man in a red suit, with horns, tail, cloven hooves, and a pitchfork. But the devil is a person. The Second Vatican Council in the *Constitution on the Church in the Modern World* uses the expression "personified evil" or "Evil One" (depending on the translation), instead of *Satan*, in explaining at what urging man, at the dawn of history, chose creature over Creator at the time of the first sin. Either Council term implies that the devil is a person.

Our Lord, when He was accused of casting out devils (Matthew, chapter 11, verse 22) by the power of Beelzebub, went along with the Pharisees in speaking of the devil as a person. Beelzebub was just a fiction, a local Canaanite god. But, in answering, Christ uses *Satan* as a personal name. Incidentally, He leads up to the frightening disclosure that there is an unforgivable sin, which can only be final impenitence like that of the personal devil.

Chapter 5 of St. Mark's Gospel (about the Lord driving the devil named Legion out of a man into a herd of swine) is typical of the Gospel writers' conviction that devils are persons.

In ancient Jewish times, evil was naively thought of as coming from God, but as revelation progressed to New Testament times it was learned that evil can come only from one source, that which is opposed to the will of God.

Philosophically, evil is simply the lack of goodness. Sin consists in not following the will of God, not in a new evil creation by one already a creature. No one can add evil to infinite good.

Papal pronouncements of the nature of the devil have not been necessary since the Christian tradition has been maintained, even by those who departed from the Church. The Muslim traditions are pretty much the same as the Jewish. Only practicing materialists are so unbelieving as not to acknowledge the existence of good and bad spirits.

Modern skepticism would have one believe that the devil, as now understood in the believing world, is just a religious abberation of the Old Testament usage of the word *Satan*, which represents the sum total of evil or the presence of evil (absence of good) in a given situation.

In Hebrew grammar, a word needs the definite article in order to be understood as a personal name. It is true that in the whole Old Testament Satan is grammatically a personal name only once (1 Chronicles, chapter 21, verse 1). But in the New Testament and fullness of revelation, *Satan* is a person, not just an abstraction.

Q. 59. What does the term Black Mass mean? Can you tell me anything about its origin or purpose?

A. Will do. Before the 1963 liturgical reforms the term *Black Mass* was often used for the daily Mass for the Dead. Many priests chose it rather than the other

Masses that could be said on days on which no feasts occurred because most of the Mass intentions were for the departed. And it cannot be denied that, if time were a factor, it could be said more quickly than the average saint's Mass. The *black,* of course, came from the required color of the vestments. Black has been discontinued as a liturgical color, so the term *Black Mass* has faded away, even though the intention of most Masses is "for the departed."

But the term has a much less innocuous meaning in connection with satanic cults. Satan worshipers are usually regarded as heathens with mental aberrations inclining them toward evil instead of good. But in medieval and recent European history, the term *Black Mass* has indicated the ghastliest act conceivable by human beings. It is not just a parody of the Mass, which would be blasphemous enough for most tastes, but requires a real priest actually consecrating for the unthinkable purpose of desecrating the Sacred Species for the insult of the Almighty. The persons involved have the gift of faith, really believe in the Catholic doctrine of the Real Presence, but are capable of the monstrous iniquity of deliberate defilement. Human sacrifice to Satan and sexual perversions are only afterthoughts to the central act. Joris-Karl Husymans in his novel, *La Bas,* told the story of the original Bluebeard of lore, along with more modern but similar satanisms, but it is very hard not to see serious mental aberration in the capering of most satanists.

CHAPTER SEVEN

MARY AND THE SAINTS

Questions on the Immaculate Conception,
the apparitions at Medjugorje,
why Catholics ask the saints to intercede,
and more.

Mary and the Saints

Q. 60. Is the Immaculate Conception celebrated as the conception of Jesus or Mary? How was the December 8 date arrived at?

A. December 8, the feast of the Immaculate Conception, was arrived at by allowing the normal nine months between conception and birth. The birthday of the Blessed Virgin traditionally was September 8, founded on a private revelation. St. Marilius in Angers, France, established a local feast of the Nativity of the Blessed Mother after a man told him that he heard angels singing in heaven that night. When he asked them why, they said it was the birthday of the Blessed Mother.

The Immaculate Conception concerns only the Blessed Mother. It means that she was different from the rest of mankind because at the instant of her conception, which was the normal result of the use of marriage by Joachim and Anna, she did not inherit original sin from them. Consequently her Son, who had no human father, could not inherit original sin

129

from her and thus become an unworthy victim in His sacrifice which was to redeem humanity.

It may be a little confusing to note here that Jesus' conception was also immaculate, that He had no stain of original sin either. The greater source of confusion lies in the mistaken assumption by uninstructed persons that the Immaculate Conception is the same doctrine as the Virgin Birth. It is not. The Virgin Birth means that Jesus was born of a virgin and had no human father. The Blessed Mother had a father and a mother and was normally conceived and born. Why two so different doctrines could be confused by otherwise very intelligent authors, commentators, and columnists is perhaps to be explained by their presumption that the Catholic Church thinks that all sex is dirty business and that the Church must be using the word "immaculate" to indicate the absence of any sex act in the conception of Jesus.

Q. 61. If the Blessed Mother is really appearing in Medjugorje, Yugoslavia, why hasn't the Church told us more about these apparitions?

A. Because the Church in general and prudent editors in particular are reluctant to set forth as established Catholic faith what is only the statement of an ordinary fallible human being or beings. People who say God spoke to them or that the Blessed Mother appeared to them may certainly be telling the truth. But there are so many of them with such conflicting messages that the Church must wait to see what the results of such private revelations will be. In the case of Lourdes and Fatima, the Church eventually approved the devotions which were rooted in what children said the Blessed Virgin told them. But approval came because the results of these apparitions were so good, not because the Church felt any obligation to listen to what pious children said.

Saints with visions get canonized but not as quickly as less spectacular saints. St. Margaret Mary (of the Sacred Heart devotion) was not canonized for two centuries, but down-to-earth St. Therese of the Child Jesus was elevated to sainthood very soon, as such things go, after her death. In speaking of visionaries in general, Catholic and Protestant, questions about their mental health must be answered, since—as both Monsignor Ronald Knox in *Enthusiasm* and William James in *Varieties of Religious Experience* have pointed out—a good many of them end up with the conviction that they are God.

Q. 62. Where do our beliefs in the Assumption of Mary into Heaven and her Crowning as Queen of Heaven come from?

A. The Assumption and Crowning of Mary are familiar to most Catholics because they are mysteries of the Rosary. They got into the Rosary from ancient Catholic traditions which originated in theological reasoning rather than texts in the Bible.

The reasoning behind the doctrine of the Assumption is that since Mary was sinless she was exempt from the penalties attached to original sin. She suffered only the penalties which Christ Himself suffered: death, for example. Physical decay of the body after death also follows from original sin, but Mary escaped this penalty, going body and soul to heaven immediately upon her death. As the only all-human person never to sin, she did not have to wait until the Last Judgment for the reunion of her body and soul after death.

The Coronation of the Virgin is a popular subject in Christian art, and most people in saying the Rosary imagine a glorious ritual in heaven in her honor. But the theological meaning of the crowning is that—since she alone of creatures was free of all sin—she is the most beautiful, glorious, and beloved creature of God. "Queen of Heaven" sums up in a title the fact that she is supreme among all the beautiful souls who have found God in glorifying and loving Him.

It should not bother you that these doctrines are not specifically expressed in the Bible. The written Bible is not the original source of the Catholic faith. That faith comes to us from the preaching of Christ and His Apostles. Christians upon receiving their faith began to think through the message that God had become a man and had had a human mother. Among the ultimate conclusions was that the Mother of God was assumed into heaven at her death and there took her place as the highest of God's creatures.

Q. 63. I can't agree with the use of the title Co-Redemptrix for the Blessed Virgin Mary. Only the cross of Christ can save.

A. The cross didn't save us, Christ did. The cross however is part of the whole process of redemption which may help to explain why some theologians give the title "Co-Redemptrix" to Mary. Without Mary, there would have been no redemption as we know it. Without Mary's consent at the Annunciation and without the utterly sinless person of Mary in the gestation and birth of Christ, there would have been no sinless God-Man capable of redeeming us.

I don't know of anyone teaching that the *co* in Co-Redemptrix means absolute equality, or that there are two redeemers acting in unison, or, blasphemously, that we are redeemed primarily by Mary. The Dogmatic Constitution of Vatican II, *Lumen Gentium*, has a chapter on the Blessed Virgin which says "... this sacred synod ... does not wish to decide those questions which the work of theologians has not yet fully clarified. Those opinions therefore may be lawfully retained which are propounded in Catholic Schools concerning her ..."

The text applies the title *Mediatrix* to Mary in another place which would indicate, let us say, that Mary has an integral part in the redemption as God Himself programmed it. So while the Church has not defined that Mary is Co-Redemptrix, it does allow the use of the term in devotional literature. Once you are given the faith to believe that Mary is the Mother of God, it is difficult not to cast about for new superlatives in her praise. You don't have to be Catholic to be so affected. The philosopher-poet George Santayana was devoted to her, even though he was said to believe that "there is no God and the Blessed Virgin is His Mother." William Wordsworth in the course of writing his anti-Catholic *Ecclesiastical Sonnets* called her "our tainted nature's solitary boast." "Co-Redemptrix" properly understood, is not too extravagant a title for Mary.

Q. 64. If Mary was without even original sin, why did she say to Elizabeth, "My spirit rejoices in God my savior"? Why would she need a savior?

A. Because she was a member of the human race. She remained all her life as Adam and Eve were before the Fall, utterly sinless. But she was a member of Adam's race and needed protection from the virus of original sin with which Adam infested his other descendants. She was preserved from original sin by the merits of Christ. All others are redeemed from (not preserved from) original sin by His merits. She needed a savior but not, strictly speaking, a redeemer.

We ordinarily use *redeemer* and *savior* in the same sense. The distinction between them is so subtle that it is only in the case of the Immaculate Conception that we need to make it. It would seem that Mary knew the distinction and spoke of her Son as her savior rather than her redeemer. The distinction is found in the basic meaning of the words *redeemer* and *savior*.

"To redeem" is to buy back something you once owned and somehow lost. Christ bought us back from the devil, who came to own us through Adam's sin. Mary never needed such buying back since she never was subjected to the devil by any sin.

"To save" basically means "to keep." Mary was kept as His own by God, not ever subjected, handed over, or lost to the devil through any sin. So, though at first sight it might have seemed to you that you had found a text in Scripture which contradicted a teaching of the Church, you wondered about it only because, like nearly everybody else, you assumed that *savior* and *redeemer* meant exactly the same thing.

Q. 65. Did Mary have other children besides Jesus?

A. No. The Blessed Mother is "ever virgin." Matthew 12:47-48 is the passage where Jesus is told His mother and brothers were standing outside asking to speak to Him. He responded with a question, "Who is My mother and who are My brothers?" He then indicated that His disciples and whoever did the will of His Father in heaven were His brother and sister and mother.

Somebody got their notes wrong here. There is no such grammatical thing as a "familial *form*" of the Greek noun *adelphoi* (brother), which is spelled identically both times it occurs in Matthew 12:47-48. It is true that those who spoke to Christ used the Aramaic equivalent of *adelphoi* in the familiar or ordinary *way*, since there was no word in their language which would distinguish blood brothers from other relatives (called "brethren" in the Catholic edition of the Revised Standard Version of the Scriptures). It is also true that Christ, in using the Aramaic equivalent of *adelphoi,* used it in a nonfamiliar or figurative sense, in saying that whoever did the will of His Father was His brother.

With all this understood, there is nothing in Matthew 12:47-48, which would negate the Catholic arguments for the perpetual virginity of Mary. These arguments are drawn from the fact that no one in the Scriptures is specifically called a child of Mary; the Blessed Mother was a virgin at the birth of Jesus (Matthew 1:20-23); she intended to remain one (Luke 1:26-35); she was commended to the care of John the Apostle by Jesus on the cross (not to the care of one of His "brothers"), and the constant tradition of the Church calls her the Blessed Virgin.

Q. 66. Is it true that Mary, being without original sin and never having sinned, had no reason to die before being taken up into heaven?

A. Correct. Mary did not have to die, since death is part of the penalty for original sin. But in the opinion of most theologians she died in order to imitate her Son. It would be more precise to say that God in His Providence had her die for this purpose rather than say she herself made the choice.

As for Elijah, the second chapter of the Second Book of Kings (used to be the fourth book) has the story of his going in a whirlwind to heaven. It doesn't say that he died nor that he did not die in the process. But in Jewish religious belief, it was readily presumed that he had not died.

He was ranked with the angels, thought to be without sin, and expected to be the man to act as high priest at the end of the world. King Joram of Judah received a letter from him apparently after the whirlwind took Elijah to heaven. While still on earth, he multiplied the food and oil of the widow of Zarephath, restored life to the dead son, called down fire on his enemies, and so on. So the belief arose that he had not died and would return as the precursor of the Messiah. The Book of the prophet Malachi closes with the promise that Elijah would be sent to the Jews before "the great and terrible day of the Lord" would come.

But it is not an article of defined Catholic faith that Elijah has yet to die, nor has any Church Council ever compared him with Mary on this point, so your question has no neat answer. There is no compelling reason why Elijah should escape the common penalty of original sin. When the saying spread among the followers of the Lord that John was not to die, that Apostle in his Gospel was careful to explain that they had mistaken a statement of the Lord. Their mistake was typical of religious enthusiasm and perhaps we should not make the same mistake about the prophet Elijah.

Q. 67. Why do we ask the saints to intercede for us when we can go right to God Himself?

A. Prayer for the intercession of the saints is not necessary to salvation. Prayer to God is—for those who know He exists. You could get to heaven without ever praying to a saint, but to act that way purposely would be out of step with the liturgical worship the Church offers to God. Saints have feast days and special prayers with their names in them and so on.

The reason the Church prays this way is that she believes in a dogma called the Communion of Saints, as recorded in the Apostles' Creed. The dogma is that the Church is made up of the saints in heaven, persons still on earth, and the temporary inhabitants of purgatory.

The bond of God with all His rational creatures is love. This is not just an emotion as some misunderstand it, but an enduring desire for the happiness and well-being of persons other than oneself. Our prayer for the intercession of the saints is an expression of belief in what the saints are doing for us—expressing desire for our supreme well-being, union with God.

The average person, praying for relief from illness, doesn't always consider the Communion of Saints as being the basis of his hope for relief—more probably he just assumes that the saints in heaven have better standing with God than anyone on earth can have, so he asks for saintly help. But there can be no objection even to that prayer. It is based, even though unknowingly, on the dogma of the Communion of

Saints, which holds that rational creatures should love each other as well as the God from whom all love comes. Praying to the saints fundamentally is a statement of our love for them and a request that they show their love by praying for us. In no way does it detract from our love or their love of God.

Q. 68. How many saints are there all together and where can I purchase a good book about the saints?

A. Start out with *Butler's Lives of the Saints,* available from Christian Classics, P.O. Box 30, Westminister, Maryland, 21157. Without being a hagiographer, I can tell you that the saints cannot be counted because it was not until 1634 that the Pope, Urban VII, reserved all further declarations of sainthood to the Holy See. Before that, local dioceses venerated deceased holy persons at the will of the people or the bishop. Nobody kept count, so even if a tireless researcher could be exact about the number of canonizations since Urban VII no total number of saints could be made.

Since formal canonizations began, saints have tended to be white Europeans. Fairly recently, the Church has realized the imbalance and has purposely canonized members of races other than the white. For instance the Uganda martyrs, led by Charles Lwanga, twenty-two in number, killed by a King Mwanga about a hundred years ago, were canonized by Pope Paul VI in 1964. The Japanese martyrs, Paul Miki and his twenty-five companions, were crucified in Nagasaki in 1597 and persons who inherited the Catholic faith from them were killed by the A-bomb there in 1945.

For a book on the early martyrs of the Church, who—so to speak—lived too soon to be formally canonized, write to Our Sunday Visitor, 200 Noll Plaza, Huntington, Indiana 46750, and ask for *The Days of the Martyrs* by C. Bernard Ruffin. I suppose that many of the stories there are "legendary," in that they cannot today be historically established. But they may do more for your faith than the stories of formally canonized, twice- and thrice-witnessed saints who lived in holiness in less exacting times.

CHAPTER EIGHT

THE POPE AND INFALLIBILITY

Questions on how many Popes
have there been,
the infallibility of the Pope,
how many Popes were married,
and more.

The Pope and Infallibility

Q. 69. How many Popes have there been?

A. Catholic historians generally say there have been 265 Popes. There is also general agreement on which were true Popes and which were anti-popes despite the complexity of the historical events. It doesn't make much difference which were which anymore as far as Catholic belief and practice go. The more important point is that the line of true successors to Peter continued somewhere in the historical maze.

The historian Lord Macaulay said of the papal succession that it goes back from the Pope who crowned Napoleon in the 19th century to the Pope who crowned Pepin in the 8th and farther back until it is lost in "the twilight of fable." It is true that about all we know of some of the earliest Popes is their names, but the Apostolic succession of Popes will undoubtedly continue even after, to quote Macauley again, "some traveler from New Zealand shall, in the midst of a vast solitude, take his stand on a broken arch of London Bridge to sketch the ruins of St. Paul's."

In determining the exact number of Popes, we have to remember that present-day historians have to use ancient lists. Those lists reflect different opinions of the compilers as to which were true Popes. Were Anacletus and Cletus really two different Popes, or the same man known by two names? Some lists included only Popes actually consecrated and omitted some who were elected but died before crowning or installation. One Pope's resignation of his claim to the papacy may have been forced. Should he be counted? John XXI should have called himself John XX, John XIV was counted twice in the *Liber Pontificalis*, and so on.

Before Gregory VII (1073) the lists by no means agree, but since his time we are pretty sure of even the dates of consecration and death of all the Popes.

Q. 70. Can you explain the infallibility of the Pope?

A. We should think of the Holy Spirit as the source of the Pope's infallibility. When Christ ascended to heaven, the Holy Spirit was sent by Him to guide His Church. The Holy Spirit, of course, does not make mistakes or lead us astray.

It is not correct to say that, in the exercise of his infallibility, the Pope can "change" doctrine. As the chief executive officer in the Church, he can command changes in things like liturgy and governmental procedure. But he could never, for instance, change the teaching that there are three Persons in God, to a teaching that there are only two Persons in God. He defines what Church doctrine is, he does *not* invent it. The last two infallible decrees were the declarations that Mary was conceived without sin (1854) and that she was assumed into heaven at her death and suffered no corruption of her body (1950). Both of these dogmas were universally held in the Church centuries before they were defined, and inquiries were made in every diocese to make sure they were.

The logical argument for papal infallibility is that Christ could not conceivably have founded a Church that would lead people into error, nor a Church that would have no means of being certain it was following Christ's doctrine. It has that means of certainty in an infallible leader, the Pope.

Q. 71. How many times has the Pope spoken ex cathedra, that is, infallibly?

A. Pius IX in 1870 declaring the doctrine of infallibility; Pius IX in 1854 defining the doctrine of the Immaculate Conception; and Pius XII in 1950 defining the doctrine of the Assumption of the Blessed Virgin Mary. That's three for sure. To that number you can add the number of canonized saints. But to count even approximately the times Popes reigning before Pius IX spoke infallibly, a researcher would have to apply the criteria set out in the decree of infallibility to every important pronouncement by every Pope since

Peter. There would be no problem in statements of doctrine which are still held as part of the tradition of the Church, nor any problems with future pronouncements of Popes who say they are speaking *ex cathedra.*

Problems would arise where matters of historical fact were uncertain and in cases like that of Galileo where the language certainly indicates that the writers thought they were agreeing with an infallible Pope. Applying the criteria of Pius IX to that case shows that infallibility was not involved. The Pope's name, Paul V, did not appear on the document of censure written by the Inquisition, and the condemnation was of a scientific matter rather than one of faith. The fact that the Pope agreed with the inquisitors and even thought a matter of faith was involved would not make the document an infallible pronouncement.

So I can't answer your question as put, but I can point out that *ex cathedra* pronouncements are rare and that the average of three in the last one hundred thirty-four years could be projected back to St. Peter to get an answer of fourteen or fifteen, if we exclude the canonization of saints.

This statement is not an implication that the rest of the teaching of the Church can be safely ignored. Even noninfallible pronouncements of the established teaching authority in the Church must be followed. If only the provably infallible decrees had to be followed, religious chaos would reasonably be expected. Infallible decisions of the future, like those of the past, will concern spiritual matters like the Assumption and Immaculate Conception, which earthly science does not deal with, much less understand.

Q. 72. Who was the first married Pope, how many were married in all, and why was the practice stopped?

A. Peter, the first of all Popes, was married. His mother-in-law is referred to, though not named, in the Bible. Mark and Luke both tell of the visit to the home of Peter by our Lord, and of His curing the fever of Peter's wife's mother.

It is hardly possible to answer how many Popes were married since historical information on many of the early Popes is scanty. The majority of the clergy lived as celibates through the first three centuries. In 386 a council in Rome made celibacy the law.

The example of Christ and the teaching of St. Paul gave the initial impulse toward celibacy to the clergy. But it was their general resolve to live a more religiously rigorous life than that of most laymen which kept their practice going.

Even the laity in those early times idealized celibacy in the practice of spiritual marriage—where a couple would live together but as a brother and sister. As we know from St. Paul (1 Corinthians, chapter 7, verse 36), the ideal was not always attainable. So, also, in the case of the clergy, Church authority was in a perennial struggle to keep the institution of celibacy. In fact, when churches have broken away from Rome, the first practical consideration always has been to abolish celibacy for the clergy.

To address your question about why the practice of having married Popes was stopped, the only answer is that it never started. There have been married Popes, but they were exceptions to the rule.

In the discipline of the Eastern Orthodox Churches, priests may not marry, but married men may be ordained priests. Adrian II, the last married Pope, was married before he was ordained (just like St. Peter).

Q. 73. I hear that Pope Benedict IX, who reigned from 1032 to 1044, was only twelve years old when he was selected to be Pope. If so, who selected him and was the Holy Spirit involved in the selection?

A. Several of the more gossipy historians of the period do say that this Pope was only twelve when he took over the papacy, but most students of the times think that twelve was a most unlikely age and that he was about twenty—which is still too young for such high office.

Before going into the question of what the Holy Spirit had to do with this election, we must consider the circumstances under which it occurred. It was a time of private armies, and bitter and bloody strife between families (comparable to our present Mafia groups) when the political or military rulers of Rome decided who was to be Pope. The free election by the cardinals of the Church, with which we are familiar, was not enacted into law until the reign of Nicholas II (1059-1061), who himself was installed by military power.

Benedict IX (Theophylact of the powerful Tusculan family) was the nephew of the two Popes who preceded him. He really gave nepotism a bad name by his immoral life and actual sale of the papal office. Driven from Rome by the citizens enraged by his excesses, he resigned the office with the arrangement that John Gratian became Pope (as Gregory VI). Gratian thought of himself as a good Pope in rising above the current use of poison and poinards to gain the office by simple purchase. There was at the time no Canon Law against this type of simony. Theophylact later tried to get the office back but was deposed along with Gratian and another claimant (Sylvester) by the Emperor Henry III. There was a book published in 1895 about the possibility that Benedict IX died doing penance at the Abbey of Grottaferrata in Italy.

As for the place of the Holy Spirit in all this, the Church has never claimed that divine guidance ensured the elevation of only pious and worthy men to the pontificate. God does not retract his gift of free will and consequently there have been Popes who were sinners and malefactors and children of their own times. Catholic teaching is that the Holy Spirit guides and supports the Church through such evil times to ultimate spiritual victory.

Q. 74. I hear Pope John XXII was a bad man. This puzzles me since the name *John* was taken by so good a Pope as John XXIII. Can you clarify this for me?

A. Not perfect, but not all bad. It is true that in modern times Popes have tended to take the name of some admired predecessor. In the case of John Paul I, the name was compounded of two predecessors of contrasting temperaments, with the implication that the differences between them could be brought into unity. John Paul II obviously concurred with this concept by taking the double name of his short-lived predecessor.

But I doubt that John XXIII had John XXII in mind when choosing his name in the papacy. John XXII was extremely ugly, very rich, and continued his predecessor's choice of the papal fiefdom in Avignon (France) as a residence rather than Rome, where he belonged.

However, he personally lived the life of a good Cistercian monk. The scandals such as nepotism and debauchery that come to mind with the words *bad Pope* or *Borgia* were not part of his career. He reigned from 1316 to 1334, during a time when there was great political opposition between the French and Italian cardinals. He was French.

Historically, his opponents went so far as to elect an anti-pope in Rome (Nicholas V, so-called) who lasted only three days before being driven away by the Roman populace. Also historically, John XXII was accused of heresy. He had said in a sermon that none of the dead enjoyed the Beatific Vision until the Last Judgment. The theologian of the University of Paris then requested that he make a public profession of orthodoxy, which he did.

He did good papal work in sending missionaries as far as Turkestan and Tartary, and he strengthened the missions in Africa, Persia, and India. He also organized a small crusade which gained several naval victories over the Turks. He tried at least twice to move the residence of the papacy back to Rome, but did not have the political power to do it. It was not until 1377 that Catherine of Siena, the saint, persuaded John XXII's fifth successor, Gregory XI, to go back to Rome from Avignon.

CHAPTER NINE

CHURCH LAWS, DEVOTIONS, AND PRACTICES

*Questions on why the Church doesn't allow
priests to marry,
why parishes allow bingo and bazaars,
why Catholics pray to the hearts of Jesus
and Mary,
and much more.*

Church Laws, Devotions, and Practices

Q. 75. Why doesn't the Church allow priests of the Latin Rite to marry?

A. The simple answer to your "Why is this so?" is that the legislation and tradition of the Church as interpreted by her legitimate lawmakers has forbidden marriage to a large percentage of the clergy for many centuries of her history.

But the underlying issue calls for a longer answer to your question. Posed as a question, that issue is the same one that was always the most frequently deposited in the question box at the parish missions of the early part of this century. It is, "Why don't (all) priests get married?"

The answer to that is more than just an observation about the law of the Church. The answer requires a look at the origins of celibacy and the motives of those who practice and encourage it.

At the bottom of the whole discussion must be the fact that Christ was not married. Theologically, He was the perfect man and so His non-marriage cannot be reasonably attributed to a physical deficiency or lack of natural physical inclination to marriage. Christ made celibacy (non-marriage) part of His natural human life.

No one claims that He was teaching that all of His followers should follow His example. But if He is to be the ideal of all Christians at least some of His believers could be expected to imitate His celibacy in their own lives.

St. Paul had no wife and counseled others to be as he was. He did not insist on celibacy for everyone, but obviously regarded it as a state preferable to marriage for those who could persevere in it for spiritual reasons. It was better to marry than to burn, he said. Recent versions read "be inflamed with passion" instead of "burn." Paul obviously means that his counsel is not for everybody. But his suggestion was widely accepted, notably by the early Christians of North Africa, among whom were the hermits who went off into the desert to live alone.

The difference between the Eastern and Western parts of the Church on celibacy of the clergy arose very early. There were no schisms over the matter, but local councils and synods of the East did not have the same strict viewpoint as the Western bishops. In Spain, for instance, in the year 300 a law was passed that clergy who were married had to give up their wives or be deposed. In the East the attitude was about the same as it is now: married men could be ordained to major orders, but, once ordained, celibate clergy could not marry.

With St. Benedict and his monks (about the year 500) monasticism and its accompanying celibacy for monks became a permanent institution with the Church, both East and West.

By the time of St. Leo the Great (A.D. 446), celibacy for the secular clergy generally prevailed in the West, although local councils often found it necessary to legislate anew. In the real Dark Ages (10th century), when the great empire established by Charlemagne was breaking up, the wealth and honor attaching it to the bishoprics was coveted by unworthy and violent men who were often successful in usurping episcopal sees. These men neither enforced nor observed the laws about clerical celibacy. They wanted the bishoprics to be hereditary, both in the income and the office to be passed on to their heirs.

In the fight to reestablish celibacy of the clergy, the weapons of the reforming Popes, like Leo IX and Gregory VII, included legislation denying the right of anyone to inherit spiritual benefices and the prohibition of sacred orders to the sons of married clergy. Gregory forbade married clergy to say Mass and the people to attend Masses such clerics offered.

Certainly, one cannot say that all laxity was either legally or morally done away with. Legislation which began with the First Lateran Council (1123) was enacted at the Fourth Lateran Council (1215) and the Council of Trent (1545), which made marriages of the clergy invalid. This legislation is still in force and is the underlying reason for any minor prohibitions, like married Eastern Rite clergy not being allowed to officiate in the United States and English-speaking countries.

Your obvious next question, must be "Why didn't they then go with Paul all the way and let those clergy who wanted to be celibate, be celibate, and those who wanted to marry, marry?"

Their reason was that they also were encouraging as vigorously as possible one of what are called the evangelical counsels.

Poverty, chastity, and obedience are not commanded, but are recommended in the Gospels as well as in St. Paul's writings. In St. Matthew's Gospel (chapter 19) is the story of the rich young man who came to Christ to find out how to gain eternal life. He was told to keep the commandments and he said he had kept them from his childhood. Then our Lord told him that if he wanted to be perfect he should sell what he had, give the proceeds to the poor, and follow Him. The young man didn't accept the invitation to poverty but was not condemned for not taking it.

In the same chapter is the counsel of chastity. This was uttered by Christ at the end of a discourse on marriage when the very practical-minded disciples observed that if they couldn't divorce unpleasant wives it would be better not to marry at all. So, while the subject was non-marriage, the Lord said that, in addition to those persons physically incapable of performing the marriage act from birth and those made incapable by men, there were those "who have made themselves eunuchs for the sake of the kingdom of heaven." The Lord was rather obviously speaking of spiritual eunuchs, persons who refrained from the marriage act for spiritual reasons.

Thus, in response to Christ's teaching, celibacy, along with poverty and obedience (the last counseled in Luke's Gospel—"He that heareth you heareth Me"), took its place among Christian customs. Poverty, chastity, and obedience are found as practices in other religions besides Christianity, so there is something natural about them. No one need conclude that a person has to be a zealous Christian to practice them.

The bishops who legislated the celibacy of the clergy did not do so in the belief that there was anything inherently wrong about a married clergy, or that marriage for them was prohibited by divine commandment, but only in the belief that Christ counseled celibacy for those who "would be perfect." That group surely should include the clergy.

Just as a Christian can be rich, married, and highly honored in the community, and still get to heaven, some priests can be rich, married, and in high office without being condemned for it. But the general sense of the faithful is that the acceptance of the evangelical counsels is the higher road for the dedicated follower of Christ. "Take up thy cross and follow Me." The shabby priest is generally more kindly thought of than one with three-hundred-dollar suits, the bossed-around assistant more sympathetically than the imperious pastor-in-charge, and if you ask most devout Catholics, the celibate over the married clergyman. Just facts of life, not really clinching arguments in favor of celibacy.

The point basically at issue is whether Christ's counsel (not command) of perfection should be legislated into a command for men undertaking to become priests.

Among the reasons of those who did so legislate is that they wished to ensure that at least some of the members of the Church should follow Christ's counsels as well as His commands. There is also the circumstance that a Church claiming the plentitude of truth should exhibit a plentitude of effort in imitating Christ.

It is still an ideal among the Eastern Churches, some of which require celibacy of bishops and recommend it for priests. Their doctrine is very close to that of the Roman Church. Celibacy is something of an ideal for the Anglican Churches which are outwardly very much like the Catholic Church. When you get down the scale as far as the Jehovah's Witnesses, who don't even believe in the Trinity and are a sect, you find some who regard celibacy as totally unnatural and even monstrous.

So, the answer to your question is: 1. Priests of the Roman Rite are unmarried because Christ was unmarried, and for spiritual reasons, they want to imitate Him. 2. Priests of the Roman Rite are unmarried because Church law requires celibacy. 3. It was imposed because the legislators thought they should require of Christ's specially dedicated followers more than Christ actually commanded and not less than He actually counseled.

Q. 76. What should I be doing to keep the Sabbath holy?

A. Follow Canon 1247 of the new Code, which says that the faithful on Sundays and holy days of obligation are bound to participate in the Mass and abstain from those labors and business concerns which impede the worship to be rendered to God, impede the joy which is proper to the Lord's Day, or impede the proper relaxation of mind and body on that day.

This is a considerable mitigation of Exodus 31:15, but of course Christians—as St. Paul so often insisted— are not bound by the Law of Moses. It is also a mitigation of what was the general understanding that no servile work is allowable on Sunday. The new Code doesn't distinguish between servile and non-servile work but between 1. work that would allow one to go to Mass, enjoy the Lord's Day, and use it for recreation; and 2. work which would prevent any of these things.

For example, it is commendable not to shop on Sunday (in the spirit of not eating meat on Friday), but it is permissible to shop as long as it does not interfere with Mass attendance and doesn't make Sunday "just another day." Going out to eat would really be part of what the new Code encourages, a celebration and enjoyment of the Sunday. Employers of cooks and waiters and bus boys have the obligation of seeing that those under them are able to go to Mass. They can hold them to work regular hours if there is real economic necessity. The Church recognized that, even on the days when it forbade "servile" work on Sunday.

Q. **77. What am I to make of stole fees—fixed amounts for Baptisms, weddings, and burials—and Mass stipends, when people ask for Masses to be said for special intentions? In Matthew 10:8, doesn't Christ forbid the acceptance of a gift for the performance of a holy act?**

A. Let's begin with background. The Lord was making it clear that his disciples were not to think of their calling as a means of making a living or of amassing wealth, as it later turned out that Judas did. It is unlikely that stole fees or Mass stipends began with the clergy refusing to perform weddings or funerals unless they were paid. It is likely that they began when spontaneous offerings would be made by the recipients of various spiritual benefits. It is likely that eventually these offerings would be regulated by fixing the fee so that the munificence of the rich would not shame the poor out of asking for spiritual benefits. It is sadly likely that here and there the spirit of Judas would enter the picture, but not that that spirit would take over entirely.

In the case of Mass stipends, whether they go to the priest or the parish, there is the consideration that there is some cost involved in providing a place of sacrifice, such as a church, or a priest to perform the physical actions, but that consideration is secondary to the point that most people seem to miss about Mass stipends. That point is that by making a money sacrifice for the celebration of Christ's sacrifice, you make that Mass your own.

If the priest or the parish do it for nothing, the merit in justice should go to the parish or the priest, not to you. Most diocesan regulations urge that Masses be said upon request for those unable to afford the stipend or for those who offer less than the usual amount. The poor can in this way share the immense spiritual satisfaction of having initiated a re-enactment of Calvary, which comes to those who can and do offer the stipend.

Q. 78. Why, if Christ drove the money-changers from the Temple, do Catholic parishes have bingo, bazaars, carnivals, and even gambling sometimes?

A. To raise money. Before appealing to Scripture against such practices it would be well to remember the situation which the Lord attacked. In his time each Jew paid a Temple tax, usually on the occasion of a visit to the Temple. People came to the Temple from all over the world and had only foreign currency which they had to exchange for the sanctuary shekels with which law required the tax to be paid. Since He called the money-changers thieves, we can take it that they were cheating the visiting pilgrims. They were also bankers, running a side-line business which had no connection with the Temple worship. They paid a percentage of their take to the priests in charge of the Temple revenues, but this money went to individuals and was not part of the Temple income.

Modern church bingo would be wrong if the parish priest hired operators to rip off the parishioners and took a part of the profits for themselves, all in the name of religion. But few, if any, church bingo games or other activities you mention involve cheating. They are not intrinsically evil as some Christian Churches have wrongly concluded. They are certainly not ideal ways of getting money for the use of the Church, which would be donation and collections as in Apostolic times. I have heard of an organization that pays all its bills that way (it is a golf club), but all the members are generous millionaires. Most parishes have to wheedle part of their income from people by providing a little innocent fun in exchange for donations.

Q. 79. Does the church still censor books?

A. There certainly are books which you may be forbidden to read. The censorship has to come from your own conscience, however. The Church no longer specifically names the books which are forbidden.

Censorship has gotten such a bad name lately that we really have to start with fundamentals to answer your questions. A lot of people think that not even your conscience should censor your reading.

Reading for Catholics used to be censored by the *Index Expurgatorius,* a list of forbidden books issued by a congregation in Rome. The liberal thinking at the Second Vatican Council resulted in the abolition of this form of censorship.

In popular reading the old Index never made much difference anyhow. Being "banned in Boston" has always guaranteed the financial success of a risque novel. The Church long ago gave up trying to put such publications out of business by forbidding Catholics to read them.

Books from the Middle Ages on were formally condemned by name because they were in error about some tenet of the faith, not because they were racy or titillating. The Church generally considered that books of the latter type were already forbidden by conscience and didn't bother to name them in the Index.

In the case of scholarly books, I think it is obvious that the Church has suffered from the loss of a handy kind of official criterion as to whether a book propounds true Catholic doctrine. Getting the still-required bishop's *imprimatur* ("let it be printed") is often ignored, and books are offered for serious Catholic reading which question such things as Christ's resurrection or His Virgin birth. In the old days, a Catholic had a place to look to find out whether a named author was for or against the traditional faith.

The Church has always appealed to conscience and to the natural law found in the heart of every man and woman. Whether one is willing to admit it or not, every person knows that law; everyone has a conscience. This natural law is found in the Ten Commandments and the condensations of them such as, "You shall love the Lord your God with your whole heart and with all your soul and with all your mind, and your neighbor as yourself," and "Love God and do what you will."

The point is that you cannot love God and your neighbor and at the same time read things that are intrinsically evil. We know what is intrinsically evil from simple examination. So however distasteful censorship may be to our liberated minds, there are books we have to fight against because they are intrinsically evil, because their main purpose is to induce readers to sin against faith or morals.

Censorship at times has had to mean more than an appeal to the natural law, just as the measures a nation at war takes have to include more than appeals to patriotism. Until Vatican II, the war with heresy had included prohibition of books and authors by name.

The basic thought behind it goes back to that old natural law and obedience to the Creator. That basic thought is evident in other efforts to impose censorship. The Jews getting the *Merchant of Venice* out of high-school curricula and Blacks *Little Black Sambo* out of the grade schools, the Moral Majority trying to suppress dirty books in the libraries are basically all calling attention to the natural law against injustice and moral perversic

Of course, liberals get big laughs when would-be censors attack classics. Of course, also, some pressure groups set up regulations under which the Bible itself would be banned. The Church has had similar difficulties since it first banned books. But it did make exceptions for students and scholars. Where no harm was done by allowing the reading of a "bad" book, the Church could allow it. Other organizations do not always have the facilities to make exceptions to their prohibitions and had to submit to intellectual ridicule.

What used to get a book banned by the Church? Properly, it was the content of the book. In fact, if a book is contrary to the Catholic faith or Catholic morals, it is still forbidden to read it, Index or no Index.

The whole purpose of creation is the glory of God, and nobody should read a book contrary to that purpose. If the reader wants to read it so that he can, by a knowledge of it, counteract it and promote the glory of God in so doing, he can now in conscience read it.

If a person wants to read a book for its pornographic content he cannot, in conscience, read it. And no one ever could have given that person permission to read it. Pornography gives no glory to God; it attempts to pervert the will.

It takes even more malice to read deliberately material one knows to be an effort to break down faith in the Church that Christ founded. It is the duty of the teaching Church to help by any means, including prohibitions and censorship, the faith of the average Christian.

Q. 80. What's the law on the need for imprimaturs in books like catechisms?

A. Canon 827 of the new Canon Law says that catechisms need the approval of the local bishop for publication. The second paragraph says that textbooks of scripture, theology, canon law, church history, or moral or religious disciplines cannot be used in elementary, middle, or higher schools unless published with the approval of competent ecclesiastical authority. The third paragraph says that all books on those topics should be submitted to the local bishop, even though they are not intended for use as textbooks.

The expressions *Imprimatur* and *Nihil Obstat* are not found in the text of either the old or new Code. They are just the strongly traditional Latin which expressed conformity with the law. The bishop writes "Let it be printed!" (*Imprimatur*) after the censor he has appointed has read the book and said, "Nothing stands in the way (of publication)," which is the meaning of *Nihil Obstat.*

The Index of Forbidden Books is no longer in force, so the *imprimatur* or rather, absence of it, is the way a Catholic of good will can get an official indication of the character of a book he has not yet read. The Church has no way of preventing the publication of books out of line with traditional doctrine, but at least it has a means of indicating which are which. Keep on checking those *imprimaturs*!

Q. 81. Can you explain why we pray to the hearts of Jesus and Mary?

A. While there is no scientific basis for believing that the physical heart is the seat, source, or origin of emotion, there is scarcely a poet in history who has not thought of the heart as the symbol of love. That thought is basic to a true understanding of prayer to the Sacred Heart.

The object of our worship is the person of Christ. We can be said nevertheless to pray to the Sacred Heart because His physical heart was what the theologians call "hypostatically" united to His human soul and divine personality. That means His heart was divine. This term goes back to the Council of Ephesus (A.D. 431). St. Margaret Mary didn't die until 1690 and the devotion is based on private revelations to her, but she committed no error theologically in directing devotion to a single organ of the body of Christ.

In these days of heart transplants and fading symbolism, it can be understood that to persons outside the faith the first impressions coming from prayer cards showing a heart in flames within the body of Jesus might be repulsive instead of devotional. To the illustrators, I suppose, the symbolism was so obvious that they never thought of the possibility of its being missed by anybody.

In the case of the heart of Mary, there can be no worship of the physical heart anymore than there can be divine worship given to her. We only worship God. In the Blessed Mother's case, any reference to her heart must be understood as being completely symbolic of her love for us and our love for her.

Q. 82. What is the Church's current teaching on indulgences?

A. Vatican Council II, in a document, *The Doctrine of Indulgences,* directed that a new list of official indulgences be drawn up and promulgated by the Church. There was no change in the Church's doctrine on indulgences or purgatory.

The new list was called the *Enchiridion of Indulgences* when it appeared. It revoked all the indulgences it did not specifically name. There are about seventy of the old indulgences thus spared, but the Church more than made up for the loss of the thousands of other indulgences by decreeing that a partial indulgence could be gained by: 1. raising one's mind to God in the performance of *any* duty or *any* patient suffering of the ills of life; 2. by *any* gift or services to persons in need; 3. by every voluntary "giving up" of anything not sinful yet pleasing to one's self. The meaning of a "partial" indulgence was not changed, it still means that part of the punishment in purgatory for already repented and forgiven sin is taken away. The old (before 1967) way of distinguishing partial indulgences by evaluating them in terms of days, months, and years was done away with, since the new emphasis was on the disposition of the mind and heart, rather than on the

exact outward recital of the prayer or precise performance of the good work involved in gaining
indulgences.

As for plenary indulgences, which remit all the
punishment for forgiven and repented sin, there are
still some listed in the *Enchiridion,* but the thrust of the
new legislation would seem to be to make them
subject to special declaration by the Pope on great
occasions or in connection with special spiritual
projects as they were in the Ages of Faith.

**Q. 83. Can't blessed palms and other blessed articles be
discarded after they have dried up and isn't there an
approved way of doing it?**

A. You bring up a perennial problem for devout Catholics. But along with broken rosaries, worn-out scap-
ulars, and uninteresting holy cards, palms can be
discarded without really offending God. They are
"sacramentals," that is, things which can dispose a
human mind toward the obedience and love of God,
but they are not in themselves "holy."

On this minor theological point the Protestants
have turned out to have been more accurate than
some of the more popular Catholic catechism writers.
Thoughts and persons can be holy because they can
give conscious honor to God. Material things can give
honor to God by their mere existence, but there is
nothing voluntary in that so they cannot properly be
called holy in themselves. I do not say that the Church
has been completely mistaken all these years, it has

only been allowing human inclinations in holding some things in special reverence because they lead the mind to God.

In secular and non-Christian circles, the reverence paid to such things as memorial statues, plaques, national emblems, and even company logos is of the same quality that Catholics give to relics and sacramentals. Reverence toward mere material objects is a human habit, not only a religious observance. The Church takes advantage of it only to bring honor to God.

Q. 84. What is the purpose of holy water, especially the practice of blessing oneself on entering and leaving Church?

A. It's done to ward off evil spirits. Let me explain the background. Water was used extensively in the Jewish, Greek, and Roman religions of ancient times, obviously because of the aptness of the washing symbol, good things being clean and *evil* things unclean.

John the Baptist used a Jewish ceremonial washing in connection with his call to penance. And our Lord in submitting to John's baptism gave to all water the spiritual power of washing away original sin in the sacrament of Baptism. Until the coming of Christ, the world was under a certain dominance of Satan, who brought on original sin. It is still being won back only gradually by the spiritual efforts of Christ's followers. So the use of holy water is a spin-off from Baptism.

The logic is that if water specially blessed can achieve such tremendous effects in the sacrament of Baptism, surely water specially blessed for other purposes will be spiritually helpful. The custom of blessing oneself with holy water on entering church symbolizes a washing away of secular things on entering the house of God. You shouldn't bless yourself on leaving.

The use of holy water by sprinkling—both in one's home and in the blessing by priests of people and things, and in the Mass—symbolizes spiritual disinfecting of disease and unclean spirits as we learn from the old prayers used in the blessing of water.

All repetitious actions are suspect of being superstitious by persons who do not know their meaning, but blessing oneself with holy water cannot be a superstitious act on the part of a Catholic who understands what he is doing. In the old list of indulgences, if I remember correctly, you got fifty days for blessing yourself and one hundred for doing it with holy water. Now, of course, you get only an unquantified partial indulgence for either action, but partial indulgences vary in quality according to the devotion of the one praying. Holy water still adds to the quality of the blessing.

Q. 85. What role do relics play in the worship of God, especially those of the True Cross and of the saints?

A. Relics are not used in the Mass or the Divine Office which make up the official worship of the Church.

They are used in devotional exercises (blessings and processions, for instance).

Time was, of course, when the veneration of relics seemed to be the chief activity of medieval Catholics, and it was one of the contributing causes of the Protestant Reformation. There was a good religious element in the public veneration of relics, but the relics became the cause of dissension and minor wars when towns fought to possess famous ones as a matter of civic pride. Traffic in relics and false relics was the chief support of many irresponsible clerics and religious establishments.

The sale, and even the transfer, of significant or famous sacred relics is forbidden by the new Canon Law as it was in the old, but devotion deriving from relics is now being played down by the Church. The word *holy* in reference to Christ's cross was removed from the liturgy. Also indulgences attached to such actions as the kissing of relics have been attached to appropriate prayers instead. And the new Canon Law—instead of specifically stating that each altar stone must enclose relics of saints (as the old Code did)—says only that the practice of keeping the relics of martyrs and other saints under "fixed altars" is to be preserved.

The Church is trying to make it plain that spiritual holiness can reside only in persons who are made in the image and likeness of the holy God, not in physical objects (which relics are). Extremists in this line of theological thought would do away even with churches and "sacred space," one of the reasons for the removal of the altar railings separating the sanctuary from the nave in so many churches. There is also the argument that our developed religion should abandon every trace of the magic and fetishes of primitive religion, which they claim the veneration of relics to be.

Pushed too far, this line of thought becomes ridiculous, since our human daily life is full of memories, souvenirs, things like memorial plaques, statues of famous men, anniversary observances, and so on—all of which are designed to stir our memory of the better things in human life.

Relics serve this same purpose and are productive of honor to God. It would be impossible to prove absolutely and scientifically that any particular relic of the True Cross is authentic, and undoubtedly many such relics are false. But I am certain that everyone upon seeing what is claimed to be a part of the True Cross is struck by the thought that this speck of wood may have touched the physical person of Christ. One thinks of His suffering and death and is the better for that thought.

Q. 86. When one lights a candle in church in memory of the dead and says a prayer does it help advance a soul from purgatory to heaven?

A. The answer is Yes, but the prayer is by far the more important action. The effect of this prayer must not be thought of as advancing a soul as one does a piece on the checker board. The Church has revised the table of indulgences so that there are now only partial and plenary (full) indulgences. Devout souls used to think mistakenly that a specific number of indulgence days were required to exactly compensate for the penalty to which the soul in purgatory was subject.

The Church, in effect, has now said it is beyond human calculation to balance good works with penalities in that way. The Church has not been wrong in the past in granting indulgences because Christ gave it that power when He said "as the Father has sent Me, I also send you." But just as no one knows the exact guilt of anyone else, so no one knows the exact quality of someone else's prayer or spiritual dispositions.

Naive persons tended to think that "forty days indulgence" meant forty days less in purgatory, but the Church never formally taught that. Forty days, for instance, meant that this indulgence was in some ways harder to win than one of seven days, and easier to gain than one of seven years. There was also the idea that these "days" were equivalent to the days of public penance imposed in the early days of the Church before readmission to the Christian Community after public sin.

Now, the Church says that *any* good deed or prayer has the same effect as the old indulgences. But since it is obvious that no one can know just how fervent the prayer was or how difficult it was for the particular individual to perform the good deed, there is no longer any point in specifying by "days" how much is accomplished in the spiritual world by our actions here in the physical world.

Q. 87. When and by whom was the Sign of the Cross introduced?

A. All we know for sure is that by the year 200 or so, the sign was widely used by Christians. Tertullian, a writer of the time, says that "whenever we come in or go out, in dressing or in putting on our shoes, at bath, or at the table, at the lighting of the lamps, in going to rest, in sitting down, whatever employment occupies us, we mark our foreheads with the Sign of the Cross."

Members of some of the cults in ancient times would mark their foreheads permanently with some sign or other indicating their membership. Christians didn't do this, but evidently they did sign a cross on their foreheads with their thumbs to indicate they were Christians and as a visible prayer act.

The next development was to make the sign with one finger to bless food. For a while the cross was made with two fingers to show belief in the two natures—human and divine—in Christ which was being denied by the Monophysites. The large Sign of the Cross from the forehead to the breast and to the shoulders was first written about by a Spanish bishop in the thirteenth century. He said it represented the progress of Christ from the Father (head) to the Blessed Virgin (mid-body or womb) to heaven (right shoulder) by way of hell (left shoulder).

It is not quite true to say the Sign of the Cross is nowhere in Scripture. After all, Christ sent His Apostles into the world to preach the gospel to every people and to baptize them "In the name of the Father and the Son and the Holy Spirit," which are the words we speak in making the Sign. The Sign of the Cross is an outward visible profession of Christian faith in the Trinity and everything the cross of Christ means.

Q. 88.What is the idea behind the adoration of the Blessed Sacrament? Is it taken from the Scripture text about the agony in the garden?

A. You are referring to a form of prayer which took its first inspiration from the words of Christ to the Apostles who fell asleep while He prayed during His agony in the garden of Gethsemane. He asked them "Could you not watch one hour with Me?" It is sentiment rather than theology which applies this text to the custom of praying in the presence of the Blessed Sacrament.

In the first ten centuries of the Church's existence, Christians considering the Eucharist thought of it as a sacrifice. They had no extra devotions outwardly demonstrating their belief that Christ was really present in the consecrated bread used as sacrifice. But they always believed that the elements of consecrated bread and wine concealed the Real Presence of Christ. They brought Communion to the sick who could not get to Mass. Hermits who lived apart from society (and did not get to Mass very often) were allowed to keep a "supply" of the Eucharist so that they could at least receive Communion. Nuns who spent time in solitary retreat after their professions were allowed to keep the sacrament for the same purpose. Bishops used to send the Eucharist to one another in token of their union in charity and faith. In the early centuries in the Eastern Church, the Mass of the Presanctified, at which there was no new consecration, only the use of the Eucharist previously confected, was enacted everyday in Lent, not only on Good Friday as we have it.

After the tenth century, the Blessed Sacrament was usually reserved in a special "casket" or house. In some places it was suspended over the altar in a dove-shaped receptacle. But the devotion such as we have now of formal, outward adoration of the Real Presence became popular only in reaction to certain Protestant denominations which denied that Christ was really present except at Communion time.

Q. 89. Whatever happened to the practice of bowing or nodding your head at the name of Jesus? Where did it originate?

A. Undoubtedly, the practice originated in the Scripture text, "At the name of Jesus every knee should bow, in heaven, on earth and under the earth" (Phil. 2:10).

Christians in general do not take this literally by kneeling at hearing the name, but recognize it by a lesser gesture of nodding. They do take it literally in supposing that St. Paul was speaking of the oral pronunciation of the name of Jesus. He was, however, using the word "name" in its ancient Biblical sense, where the "name of God" was just a variation of "God

Himself." To love, praise, and exalt the name of God is to love, praise, and exalt God Himself.

Among Jews, the sacred name of God (Yahweh) is never uttered, and when it occurs in Scripture reading, the words "the Lord" are spoken instead. Until recent times, Catholics—specifically priests in sermons and teachers in catechisms—followed the same rule about the holy name of Jesus, substituting "our Lord" or "the Lord" when it occurred in the sermon or lesson.

But in the last century the rationalist interpreters of the Bible used the human name, Jesus, invariably, to show their belief that He was only man and not God. Since He was truly man, priests and teachers thought it good to do the same in confuting rationalists, and began to refer to Him without each time proclaiming His divinity by substituting "our Lord" or "the Lord." Consequently, the holy name was spoken so frequently that the practice of recognizing it by a nod or bow (much less a genuflection) was much diminished.

It should, of course, be resumed. The indulgences attached to this reverence of the holy name are still in force. Nodding at hearing it is a good act of prayer, even though you can no longer measure or weigh the indulgence in terms of days.

CHAPTER TEN

MARRIAGE, ADULTERY, ANNULMENT, AND TEST-TUBE BABIES

Questions on the "Pauline Privilege,"
excommunication if divorced
Catholics remarry,
Jesus' treatment of adultery in the Gospels,
annulment, and test-tube babies.

TEN

Marriage, Adultery, Annulment, and Test-Tube Babies

Q. 90. What exactly is the "Pauline Privilege"? Does it mean that a Catholic can marry someone who was divorced?

A. The explanation begins with a text from Scripture found in Paul's First Epistle to the Corinthians (chapter 7, verse 12) where he discusses marriage. The key words are "... if the unbelieving partner desires to separate let it be so, in such a case the brother or sister is not bound."

Let's take a hypothetical case. Say a man is married before he was baptized to a woman who was also unbaptized. Upon his Baptism, his first wife is unwilling to live in peace with him or is unwilling to live with him at all. Thus, when she leaves him, he is no longer bound in conscience by his civil marriage to her, according to this text of St. Paul.

A sacramental marriage in the Catholic Church dissolves the former bond of marriage between unbaptized persons, so there is no bigamy. In civil law the man would have had to obtain a civil divorce, and in this sense you did witness the marriage in the Catholic Church of a divorced man.

Before the newly baptized person can enter a Catholic marriage, his or her partner in the pagan marriage must be asked whether he or she wishes to receive Baptism (in which event their marriage would become one between two believers and could not be dissolved) and whether he or she wishes to depart or live in peace in the first marriage. In Paul's time the Christians were in a tiny minority as they are in pagan parts of Africa and Asia now. The privilege he wrote into his Epistle would be used more in those situations than in Christianized areas.

Q. 91. I understand that the Pope in 1977 removed an 1884 law which automatically excommunicated U.S. Catholics who married again while in a presumed valid marriage. What are the ramifications of this and what was the original intent of the 1884 law?

A. A plausible guess at the motives of the legislators of the 1884 law would be that since they were dealing with immigrant Catholics who were subjected for the first time in their lives to the secular customs of other peoples, they wanted to teach them what the natural law was by imposing an ecclesiastical law on them which they could understand. In Catholic countries excommunication had its social effects as well as effects on conscience. That may answer another of your questions as to the benefits of its removal in recent times. Excommunication no longer has much coercive social effect or brings much public shame.

But this 1977 removal does not allow divorced remarried Catholics to receive Communion. Remarriage is on the conscience as a matter of natural law, not of ecclesiastical prohibition. In Canon Law, excommunication is a censure (not much different from what the U.S. Senate gave Joe McCarthy), that is, an expression of disapproval and a calling upon members of the Church to reject the offender.

This rejection has Biblical precedent. Our Lord in Matthew's Gospel (chapter 18) tells His followers that one who will not listen to the Church should be treated like a Gentile and a tax-collector (heathen and publican in the old versions). Most of the automatic excommunications of the 1918 Canon Law were excluded from the present 1983 Code. As in the case of the 1977 removal of excommunication, this was done in the hope that people would see that the acts for which excommunication was imposed were sins already. It was not a case of the Church deciding to make sins out of innocent actions.

Q. 92. With the woman caught in adultery in the Bible who was in danger of being stoned to death, why wasn't the man involved accused as well as the woman? Was adultery acceptable for males but pun-

ishable by death for females? Why didn't Jesus say anything about this injustice?

A. I can't presume to specify the motives of the Lord, but I can refer you to the Old Testament background of this whole incident. Adultery was *not* "acceptable" for males since the Sixth Commandment applied to both sexes. But in the social structure of the time woman was a chattel or possession; divorce was a male prerogative; and the polygamy of the patriarchs was a lingering tradition.

These injustices, please do not mistake me, were in the social structure and not in the teaching of Jesus. Our Lord's preaching, it has always seemed to me, was for religious reform—sincerity in the worship of the Father—rather than social reform, despite the obvious room for social improvement. If everyone had good religious motives in everything he or she did, there would be no injustices in the social order. So Christ did not attack the tyranny of the Romans, did not undertake to redistribute the wealth, nor correct the inequities of the social order, not even the unjust subjection of women in the society in which He lived.

But He did put to shame the male adulterers who were about to stone the female adulterer. The Lord's policy was to apply His moral corrections to what we might call individual sins as opposed to collective sins of the society in which He lived. So, rather than criticize even implicitly the procedures of Christ, maybe we can learn from Him that the true source of all evil is individual sin.

Q. 93. When did the Church start annulling marriages? Is there anything in the Bible about annulments? If a person marries after an annulment and the new marriage doesn't work out can a second or third marriage be annulled?

A. Let me take your questions in reverse order. There is no limit to the number of annulments one person can be granted, but you must remember that it isn't a question of the marriage "working out" but of whether there was a valid marriage. When you say "marriage annulment" at any time you are being inexact. The decree is really a "declaration of nullity," a judgment that there never was a valid marriage. Canon Law 1141 states that a ratified and consummated marriage can be dissolved by no human power.

As for the Bible, in cases where two pagans were married, and then one became Christian (baptized) and the pagan party wanted to abandon the marriage, St. Paul (1 Corinthians 7:15) said the Christian was no longer bound by the marriage vow. The Church goes along with St. Paul, of course, but the concept of divorce or dissolution of an admittedly valid marriage, as found in the Law of Moses, was changed by Christ Himself (Mark 10:9). So, if you use exact language, the Church never did begin annulling marriages but has always claimed the right to judge their validity, because in the Catholic faith marriage is a sacrament.

The reason you have only lately begun to hear so much about declarations of nullity is a paragraph in the 1983 Code of Canon Law (Canon 1095) which specifically states that "causes of a psychic nature" make some persons incapable of assuming the essential obligations of matrimony. That is to say their marriage contracts are invalid. In the old Code of 1918 there was no such emphasis on this possibility of invalidity. Fraud, force, and fear were considered the standard, if not the only, reasons for a declaration of nullity.

Q. 94. What does the Church teach about test-tube babies and surrogate mothers?

A. *Surrogate* in the dictionary means "substitute." It can have at least two more specific meanings when joined to the term *mother*. 1. If a woman becomes a mother with the husband of another woman and surrenders the baby to the husband and wife for a fee, she is a surrogate mother but also has been guilty of adultery. 2. If a woman allows the use of her body to bring to term the ovum of another woman already fertilized by the other woman's husband, she would not necessarily be guilty of adultery and would be a surrogate, but not really a mother. The child would be the offspring of the persons whose ovum and seed were used.

Test-tube babies involve the same set of principles. There would be no wrongdoing in assisting the union of the ovum and seed of a husband and wife. When this is done outside the body of the mother, a question of right and wrong arises from the danger to the life of the person conceived. Experimenters who do not believe that human life begins with conception are careless about such lives in their pursuit of successful conception. The latest statistic I have read says that only 7 percent of such conceptions survive to birth. A doctor who believes he is dealing with human lives could hardly feel justified in promoting such conceptions, where the price is fourteen to fifteen lives for one test-tube baby.

CHAPTER ELEVEN

THE PROPHECIES OF NOSTRADAMUS AND TWO MODERN SECTS

*Questions on what the Church says about
the prophecies of Nostradamus,
whether devout Mormons can be
considered Christians,
and information on the Jehovah's Witnesses.*

The Prophecies of Nostradamus and Two Modern Sects

Q. 95. What does the Church say about the prophecies of Nostradamus?

A. The works of Nostradamus were put on the Index of Forbidden Books in 1781. Of course, the Index has now been abolished, but this indicates the stand of the Church on his predictions and prophecies.

He probably was a practicing Catholic. But in the French society in which he lived, everybody—whether a true believer or not—was a Catholic in name at least. His conscience, whether he was inwardly devout or not, is for nobody to judge.

Nostradamus was the chief astrologer to Catherine de Medici, who ruled France as mother of three kings and who may have been responsible for killing all those Protestants on St. Bartholomew's Day in 1572. Astrologers, in those days, usually outweighed all other officials of state in royal courts when decisions were made. Astrologers were consulted even by the Popes of the time, Sixtus IV, Julius II, Leo X, and Paul III, to name just those we are sure of.

To see how this could be, you have to realize that astrology was the king of the sciences in those days. Even Kepler, the father of modern astronomy, practiced it. Copernicus, the first to say the earth went around the sun and not the sun around the earth, thought of astronomy as only a tool for better astrology. Nostradamus, as we would say today, wrote the book. His work (published in 1555) was the greatest authority on astrology.

You also have to realize that science as we know it hardly existed at the time. By *science* we mean a vast accumulation of facts founded on physical experiments which now explain all but a few natural phenomena such as black holes in space.

The astrologers had no such background. They would notice changes in the color of the moon, for instance, but not know that they could be accounted for by moisture in the atmosphere, dust storms from volcanoes on the other side of the earth, and so on. They thought the moon really changed color and that they could predict the weather from the color changes. They were right half the time, too. Predicting the weather was bread and butter work for the astrologers and formed an important branch of their "science."

But emperors, Popes, and ordinary mortals all had a desire to know more about the future than just how rainy or dry it would be. Astrology's chief interest was in the romantic, physical, or financial future of individual persons.

The theory was that the planets and star constellations influenced the person according to their position at the moment of his or her birth. The planets included the sun and the moon which could be either good or bad. Jupiter and Venus were definitely good influences and Saturn and Mars definitely bad. The remaining planet, Mercury, was a toss-up.

The signs of the Zodiac were connected with the health of various parts of the body. Aries, for instance, governed the head, and Libra the intestines. The heavens were divided into twelve "houses," and the position of your planets in one or other of the houses as you were born determined your quality of life: wealth or poverty, parentage and children, health or sickness, marriage success or failure, and time of death. Now all this was predicted on the basis—one can only suppose—of previous successful guesses, since there was positively no scientific evidence to appeal to. After a while an enormous amount of data was assembled and the individual astrologer took it from there.

Since they had no other way of learning what they wanted to know, people evidently thought that a good astrologer could dig through this haystack of possibilities and find the needle of the true future. An astrologer was comparable to a computer expert in our day. He needed just as much study and preparation and enjoyed the same unquestioning confidence in the results he obtained.

As long as astrology represented to most people the sum total of human wisdom there were not many objections to it. But when other kinds of knowledge, based on more scientific experiments, began to accumulate, astrologers began to lose their preeminence.

About the same time it began to dawn on theologians that there was something dogmatically wrong about the very basis of astrology. It was fatalistic, that is, it left no room for the human person's free will in God's creation. If all the details of your life were determined by the position of your stars at the time of your birth, there was no point in trying to avoid sin. According to traditional Catholic doctrine, human beings were obliged by God's law to avoid sin. Theologians began to condemn astrology.

Then, too, there was the point about knowledge of the future. It was obvious that human beings could figure out some of the things that would happen to them in the ordinary course of events—that the sun would rise, that everyone would die, and so on. But when it came to such things as the exact time of death, the new experimental sciences were able to show that the influences, the conditions, and the governing circumstances were so many that it was beyond the ability of any human person's mind to know them all—this kind of future one could never know. Only an infinite God could know the nearly infinite number of causes that entered into the most ordinary human or natural events.

Astrology attributed to a mere mortal, more precisely to the astrologer, knowledge that could be only God's. You see, even when you say that there are future things that humans can know, we don't know any of them "for sure." If the world comes to an end tonight, the sun will *not* rise tomorrow. It may be that some of the living at that time may *not die* but be taken alive to judgment. The Church hasn't defined anything about it.

The only human beings ever to know the future "for sure" were God's prophets when they were foretelling the coming of the Messiah and some of the things that were to happen to Him. So the astrologers were taking on themselves the gifts of prophecy which God had given to His prophets of Old Testament times. Christ Himself on the road to Emmaus appealed to the fulfillment in His life of the Scriptural prophecies as proof of His Messiahship. But astrologers claiming knowledge of the future were blasphemously claiming divine inspiration.

So astrology, which once was the guidance of Popes and emperors, has since fallen from popularity and is no longer taken seriously by people with Judaeo-Christian beliefs.

Even in our own society, there is a hard core of superstitious people. At least there are enough of them to keep those newspaper horoscopes appearing. The one I have at hand has such nuggets of wisdom as "Any rotten apple will spoil the whole barrel. Avoid wanting to get even. You may overwork. Get rest, spend time at home alone." All this in case your birthday is in Taurus, April 21 to May 21. I also have at hand a magazine advertisement for a hand-held astrological computer, a four-function calculator by which 16 combinations of personality traits are matched to the stars of any day in your life to help you in your personal relationships with your wife or boss.

But what of the possibility that most of Nostradamus' predictions have been fulfilled? That could be true, but only to somebody who has already decided what those predictions were about. The First World War or Second World War could fulfill the prediction of a "river of blood." So could a conflict between two uncivilized tribes in New Guinea if the interpreter of the prophecy happened to live nearby.

Nostradamus' prophecies were written in poetic quatrains, and in translating the sixteenth-century language, it is hard to arrive at a coherent literal meaning for the verses. Without recourse to your own imagination, it is impossible to find in them specific names, places, and dates for future specific events.

It must be a lot of fun figuring out the "predictions" in the obscure lines. As a puzzle, it has the same fascination as those impossible *London Sunday Times* crosswords in which, for instance, the clue for a five-letter word might be "an article, possibly." The answer is "thief," arrived at by finding the letters for *the* (article) and *if* (possible) in *thief.*

That's an easy one. Some of the clues are obscure, even after you know the answer. For instance, the clue, "Deputy selected in San Paulo cumulative vote" has "locum" for an answer. Get it?

Explanation: *locum* is short for *locum tenens* which is

Latin for "deputy." If you studied the clue as hard as you were supposed to, you would have seen that the last two letters in *Paulo* and the first three letters of *cumulative* form the word *locum,* so the answer was right there staring you in the face. Nostradamus' predictions are like that. After you know the answer, after each event has happened, it seems as though anyone could have understood the prediction and foreseen the answer.

One of the frustrations for Nostradamus fans must be the built-in ambiguity. He writes, "At the rising of the sun, a great fire shall be seen, noise and light tending to the north and all round about—death and cries shall be heard...." Japan is the Land of the Rising Sun and it was there that the great fire of the atomic bomb exploded, bringing death all around. But the eruption of Krakatoa was noisier and more powerful. And maybe he meant Mount Pelee or even Mount St. Helen's. It seems more likely to me that he was working out an astrological problem, couldn't decide exactly what to say, and left his options open.

Even though coincidences can be amazing, I don't see any reason for thinking that there is supernatural knowledge in the works of Nostradamus. I'll grant you that as a source of entertainment his puzzles are superb, but no one should be afraid of the horrendous "things to come" which his fans may discover in his prophecies.

Q. 96. I find the view that Mormons cannot be considered Christians offensive since I am a convert from Mor-

monism and my parents are devout Mormons. They ensured that I received a thoroughly Christian training as a child. What do you say?

A. I could agree with you, but only after adopting your meaning for the word *Christian*, which I won't do. "Christian" to many people has come to mean only "good" and "moral," indicating that goodness which is natural to human beings and which does not derive from theological beliefs. This usage was made famous by the United Nations diplomat who asked the Muslims and the Jews why on earth they could not settle their differences in a Christian spirit. They could, of course, if "Christian" meant only "kindly, sincere, honest, loving, good, moral" and so on. It's all a question of semantics. On that level, I would argue that "Christian" should be reserved for those who accept not only the moral teachings of Christ, but also the stunning revelations that He was the Son of God, equal to God the Father who came to give men and women a specific means (the Church) of attaining a blessed and eternal union in God.

The name "Christian" was first given to Christ's followers in Antioch not because of their moral goodness but because they *believed in what Christ revealed. Those who did not believe* all that Christ revealed were not called Christians. So, saying that Jews, Muslims, or Mormons are not Christian does not imply that the members of these religions cannot be as morally good as Christians. On their own principles, they should reject being called Christians, just as I would reject being called Muslim, even though the good Muslim who called me that meant it as a compliment.

We are all a little bit like the Red Queen in *Alice in Wonderland* and expect people to give words the same meaning we give them, but that procedure does not lead to better understanding of anything.

Q. 97. Can you tell me about Jehovah's Witnesses? How do they differ from Catholics?

A. They practice an aggressive type of door-to-door missionary effort which they feel is part of being a Witness, since all members who have received their non-Trinitarian baptism are considered ministers.

The sect was founded in the late nineteenth century by Charles Taze Russell, who previously had been in succession a Presbyterian, a Congregationalist, and an unbeliever. He then claimed to have had some kind of religious experience which gave him a sense of mission that he has evidently passed on to his followers.

The main emphasis in Witness doctrine is a very distorted interpretation of the Bible, which they claim as the sole source of religious belief without accepting or using any of the Jewish and Christian background of the Sacred Scriptures. They deny the doctrine of the Trinity, think that Christ was once an angel, and routinely discredit the claim of any other faith to any religious authority. They set themselves apart from even the secular community on such points as patriotism and reverence for the flag.

They do a relatively enormous amount of pamphleteering and religious publishing, none of which has any standing in intellectual or scholarly Biblical circles.

I do not mean to imply by all this that the Witnesses are social monsters. They can be very friendly and kindly people. Yet not a month goes by but what I get a sorrowing letter from some Catholic mother or father who has lost a child to the persuasiveness of the Witnesses. I can't believe that any Catholic who knows and understands his faith can be attracted by the doctrines of Mr. Russell. But it is all too evident that Christians who are passive in their religious practice can be taken in by the combination of missionary zeal and friendliness the Witnesses are so good at.

CHAPTER TWELVE

SOME THEOLOGICAL AND PHILOSOPHICAL QUESTIONS

*Questions on what God was doing
before He created everything,
whether God's knowledge of everything
takes away our free will,
what would have happened if Adam and Eve
hadn't sinned,
the Nazi holocaust,
and the human soul.*

TWELVE

Some Theological and Philosophical Questions

Q. 98. What was God doing before He created everything?

A. Nothing. He could have been just thinking and loving. (God is three Persons who love each other.) We really don't know what went on before the creation of the world except that God was perfectly happy and was so good that He wanted to share the life and happiness of His three Persons. So He made the world with us in it.

Before creation, God could have been planning what it would be like. When you think just of our bodies (so complicated that there are things with independent lives inside the tiny cells of which we are made) or the distances to the farthest-away stars that we can find by radio (billions upon billions of miles), it seems likely that God was planning creation from all eternity.

He had a lot of things to decide. Should He make us like Himself so that we could do what we wanted (even though what we wanted to do might be wrong)? Or should He make us like the animals which have to do exactly what God dictates? Should He become a man Himself so that in case human beings did sin, He could suffer the punishment instead of them?

You asked what God was doing before He made the world. I had to say "nothing" because I couldn't possibly imagine what God is or does apart from this world. But I knew it was "nothing" that anybody could understand. The real answer to your question is that in God there is no "before" or "after" only "now." We can't imagine that. It's like a square circle or a stick with only one end. Don't be disappointed if you can't understand time and eternity. Just say to yourself that God knows all about it and that you will know more about it when you get to heaven.

Q. 99. If Christ knows who is going to heaven and who to hell, doesn't that take away our free choice?

A. He does. But it is not His will but ours that makes the difference. There have been people who believed in what is called predestination, that God from all eternity made some people to go to heaven and some to hell no matter how they lived. That belief *is* "un-Catholic." It takes no account of the revelation made to humanity through Christ and the Bible which tells us that God loves all His creatures—enough to become man and suffer and die for them.

If we use only our reason and not revelation, it does seem impossible to see how God could grant free will to creatures of His and still not be responsible for them hurting themselves by sin, since He made them in the first place. Thousands of theologians through the centuries have argued about how to answer the problem. But answering it is like answering the question "Can God make a stone so big he can't lift it?" Whether you say Yes or No, you are denying that God can do everything.

Your problem is really two questions: 1. Can God be so just He ceases to be merciful? and 2. Can God be so merciful He ceases to be just? Our answer to both questions must be first Yes, on second thought No, and on third thought, "Human reason cannot answer Yes or No." But that response does not have to mean that we reject an infinitely merciful and just God. Our human reason is only finite and unable to cope with the idea of God being infinitely just while infinitely merciful.

Q. 100. What if Eve had not disobeyed God in the Garden of Eden? What would then have been God's plan for Adam and Eve and their descendants on this earth? Would there then have been any purpose in Jesus Christ coming to this planet?

A. If neither Adam nor Eve had sinned, the human race would have lived in a state of happiness until the end of the world. Since death is the penalty of original sin, nobody would ever die. Speculation leads to the conclusion that God would finally take everybody to heaven, since He had raised humans to a supernatural level after their creation. Adam was the head of the human race, so if he had not sinned and only Eve had sinned, only the guilty Eve would have been punished. But if Eve had not sinned and, as a result of her fidelity, Adam also retained his innocence, there would have been no need for the Redeemer, Jesus Christ.

The prospect of a world without Christ is as appalling to the Church as the fact of Adam's sin. So in the prayers of the Easter Vigil she calls Adam's sin a "happy fault" (*felix culpa*), as though it were a good thing that Adam sinned. The poet Edwin Muir expressed the same idea: "What had Eden ever to say/Of hope and faith and pity and love?...Strange blessings never in Paradise/Fall from these beclouded skies."

The Creator allowed Himself to be offended so that He could reveal Himself to His creatures in His Son, the Christ, in whose image and likeness the redeemable creatures were made.

Q. 101. After doing some reading, I just can't understand how God could have allowed the Nazi holocaust.

A. Your sympathy for the Nazi victims makes an eloquent statement of the problem of evil, a central element in everybody's life. The problem has not been solved in philosophy or natural theology, and even in

God's revelation one finds an answer only if one has faith.

Only faith will tell you that in spite of the suffering and death in this world, God is all-good. Many persons of high intellect but not faith—faced with the problem of evil—say either there is no God or that God is not all-good and doesn't love us.

Now, revelation tells us that God made us in His own image and likeness with free will. This free will in God's creation can oppose itself to His. All moral evil comes from that. If no one had ever opposed his human will to that of God there would never have been sin, suffering, or death.

But if God had never given human beings the gift of free will, all creation would be pointless. God's eternal love and happiness would never have been shared in any meaningful way beyond the Trinity itself. And there would be no human love of God or of human beings. We would be like the plants and animals, without any sensitivity to love as we now know it, and unlovable by God since we could not return His love.

That's about as far as anyone can go in explaining all human agonies, mental and physical, and even the death and suffering of the God-Man Christ.

Q. 102. How does the Church define the human soul?

A. As a "principle" by which we think, feel, use our free will, and have life. *Principle* is an abstract term and it may be easier to understand it if we say that the soul is "whatever-it-is" that makes us feel, think, will, and live. The body is a collection of chemical elements. Some are combined in ways so complicated that they are called "organic," meaning they are found in living things. This name distinguishes them from simple iron, calcium, hydrogen, and oxygen. But alone or combined, chemicals do not produce life. Life comes only from life. That "whatever-it-is" that makes the difference between inert chemicals and a living creature is called its soul. Even plants and animals have souls in this sense.

But human beings have human souls which, in addition to more life, give them the power to think, feel, and exercise free will. According to the Catholic Church, this human soul will never die. It begins by the special creation of God at the time of physical conception. It can exist without the living body with which it began. It had no existence prior to conception. It can experience joy and sorrow but not physical pain because it is spiritual. It can obey God or sin despite the influences its body may have on it.

The soul is not what is usually called the "mind," which is only the operating of one of the body's organs, the brain. You could have a brain transplant with no exchange or loss of your soul.

The human soul and body are each "incomplete" substances; neither one alone can make up a human person. At death the body suffers corruption, but the body will be restored and reunited with the soul at the Resurrection of the Dead.

This concept of the soul is the pivotal difference between the Church and the unbelieving materialistic world. Without the concept, human life is a meaningless puzzle, best stated by Ernest Dowson:

> They are not long,
> the days of wine and roses;
> Out of a misty dream
> Our path emerges for a while,
> then closes
> Within a dream.